Manage Your Problems

The Gopal Bhand Way

Vishal Goyal

V&S PUBLISHERS

Published by:

V&S PUBLISHERS

F-2/16, Ansari road, Daryaganj, New Delhi-110002
☎ 23240026, 23240027 • *Fax:* 011-23240028
info@vspublishers.com • www.vspublishers.com

Online Brandstore: amazon.in/vspublishers

Regional Office : Hyderabad
5-1-707/1, Brij Bhawan (Beside Central Bank of India Lane)
Bank Street, Koti, Hyderabad - 500 095
☎ 040-24737290
vspublishershyd@gmail.com

Follow us on:

BUY OUR BOOKS FROM: AMAZON FLIPKART

ISBN 978-93-815885-5-0

New Edition

Printed at : Param Offsetters, Okhla, New Delhi–110020

Dedicated

To

My Mother and Father

The Masters of Profound Wisdom

Contents

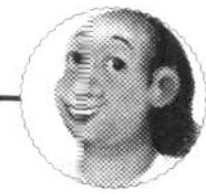

Acknowledgements

No one walks alone on the journey of life. So, perhaps this book and its pages will be seen as "thanks" to the tens of thousands of you who have helped me, joined me and walked beside me all along the way continuously urging me to put my thoughts down on.

Among the many people who helped me with this book, my special thanks to my parents for encouraging me and showing keen interest in the progress. Above all, I want to thank my brothers, my wife and rest of my family, all of whom, in their own ways inspired me and subconsciously contributed a tremendous amount to the content of this book. My son Aryan, who at his tender age sacrificed many hours which we could have spent together.

I am grateful to Sh. Sahil Gupta, Director of V&S Publishing for having great confidence in me and enabling me to publish this book. I am truly thankful to Sh. Dibya Borah, Executive Editor, for giving the final shape to this book with beautiful illustrations and pleasing cover which in itself speaks a lot. V&S Publishers is an amazing organisation comprising talented individuals who shared their knowledge, their ideas, and numerous tips all of which culminated in the completion of this book.

Last and not least: I beg forgiveness of all those who have been with me during the course of completion of this book and whose names I have failed to mention.

--- Vishal Goyal

Acknowledgements

Prologue

India's extraordinary history is intimately tied to its geography. A meeting ground between the East and the West, it has always been an invader's paradise, while at the same time its natural isolation and magnetic culture allowed it to adapt to and absorb many of the peoples who penetrated its mountain passes. No matter how many Persians, Greeks, Chinese nomads, Arabs, Portuguese, British and other raiders had their way with the land, local Hindu Kingdoms invariably survived their depredations, living out their own sagas of conquest and collapse. All the while, these local dynasties built upon the roots of a culture well established since the time of the first invaders, the Aryans. In short, India has always been simply too big, too complicated, and too culturally subtle to let anyone empire dominate it for long.

The Indian history has variety which is its special hallmark. Underneath its history, lies the continuity of Indian civilisation and social structure from the very earliest times until the present day.

During medieval India, a prominent Hindu Kingdom was **Krishnanagar,** also called Krishnagar, named after **Raja Krishna Chandra Rai**. It is located in Nadia District of present day West Bengal State, lying on the banks of River Jalangi. An important centre for culture and literature, it contained the residence of Raja Krishna Chandra Rai.

The Krishnanagar (Nadia) Empire included the present day prominent city of Nabadwip meaning "9 islands" in Bangla. Being the birth place of Sri Chaitanya Mahaprabhu, Nabadwip is a pilgrimage city and had been a great centre of learning and intellectual prowess to be aptly referred to as "Oxford of Bengal". Other well-known towns of Kalyani, Ranaghat, Kaliganj, Birnagar and Tehetta were also a part of the Krishnanagar Empire.

During the 18th century (1710-1783), Krishnanagar (Nadia) was ruled by Raja Krishna Chandra Rai, son of Raghuram Rai. Raja Krishna Chandra was an able Ruler and an Administrator par excellence. The Empire flourished under the rule of Raja Krishna Chandra Rai.

The 18th Century was a time of political turmoil and instability in *Bharat*. The Mughal Empire declined after the death of Aurangzeb (the last Sultan of Delhi Sultanate) under the later Muslim Rulers, i.e. Bahadur Shah Zafar and so on, and the *Maratha* Empire (*Marathas* are an Indian caste found predominantly in Maharashtra) was rising. In Bengal, however, the Muslim governor became independent and the *Nawabs* flourished.

At that time, the *Marathas* spread terror in Bengal especially amongst the *Nawabs* through their constant raids and *Bargi* invasions (large scale plundering by armed *Maratha* horsemen). The *Nawabs* usually sought the help of Bengali Hindu Rajas. Raja Krishna Chandra realised that Muslim power was on the wane and a new era was going to start. He always wanted to revive the Hindu Rule.

At first, the relation between Krishna Chandra and *Nawab* Alivardi Khan was cordial. But things changed when *Siraj-ud-Daula* (grandson of Alivardi Khan) became *Nawab* of Murshidabad. Raja was sad to see the suffering of Hindus during the reign of Siraj especially the Hindu women.

Nawab Siraj-ud-Daula of Murshidabad remained a constant nuisance for the Raja. He collaborated with *Robert Clive* (a British officer who established the military and political supremacy of the East India Company in Bengal. Together with Warren Hastings, he was one of the key early figures in the creation of British India) against Siraj, thus hastening the downfall of Siraj in the Battle of Plassey. Again during the time of *Mir Kasim*, Krishna Chandra was imprisoned and sentenced to death. But the British helped to secure his release with whom he maintained cordial relations.

Raja Krishna Chandra is still remembered for providing relief to Hindus besides leaving his mark in field of literature, art and architecture. Krishna Chandra Rai was proficient in Bangla, Sanskrit and Persian and during his reign, the Bengali literature developed. He was known for his public welfare activities. His wife, Rani Bhabani, was also a patron of Sanskrit culture in Bengal. He established a large Shiv temple at *Shivnibash*. He was the first to introduce *Jagaddhatri Puja* in Bengal.

Like King Vikramaditya, he too, maintained a *Navaratna Sabha* (Royal Court with Nine Jewels) which included men of letters like poet Raygunakar Bharatchandra, Ramprasad Sen, Pandit Baneswar Bidyalankar, Krishnananda Bachaspati, Jagannath Tarkapanchanan and Hariram Tarkasiddhanta and the famous **GOPAL BHAND**.

Gopal Bhand, the barber, was a simpleton but a witty village barber who spent his early days in extreme poverty. He later became the *chief jester* at the *Rajbari* (royal court) of Raja Krishna Chandra. Gopal was immensely clever and wise, entertaining the Raja and imparting wise lessons by telling anecdotes, parables and stories appropriate to the issues at point. Gopal was a genius and the King considered him to be 'gem' of his Court just like Sultan Akbar considered Birbal and Raja Krishnadeva Raya took Tenali Raman to be. Not only did Gopal entertain the King and the courtiers with his unusual wit, but he often helped the King with unexpected advice when no one else could. Gopal was given great freedom of speech. For these reasons, Gopal Bhand could be described as the *Birbal of Bengal*. His native shrewdness enabled him to turn every situation to his advantage.

He was favoured by Raja Krishna Chandra and whenever the eccentric *Nawab Siraj-ud-Daula* of Murshidabad gave Raja an impossible assignment, it was Gopal who came to the Raja's rescue. Being the Raja's favourite, however, did not turn his head. He mingled freely with the common people and often helped them too to solve their problems. That explains the popularity of this folk-hero to this day.

Gopal's concise observations concern people from all walks of life – the common man, beggars, Kings, landlords, the clergy, scholars, the trading class, warriors and others. In most of his tales, the fish – the favourite cuisine amongst Bengalis, had been his cherished subject matter.

Gopal's witty tales usually contain some hidden meaning or moral and can be interpreted at various levels. His anecdotes are now being spun in modern avatars, however, this book deals with his tales of yore right from his vagabond childhood days through his initial days of struggle to the *Rajbari*.

In one story, there was a rich farmer who grew watermelons in his field. Every day, the vagabond Gopal with other village boys would pluck his watermelons. To scare them away, the farmer put a sign in his field: "There is a poisoned watermelon in this field."

He felt sure that now his watermelons would be safe and was proud of his bright idea. The next day, when he came back, he saw that none of the fruits were missing but there was another sign kept in the field which read, "Now there are 'two'!" Gopal just reciprocated with his 'Tit for Tat' idea.

The book starts with Gopal's ***P.R.O.B.L.E.M*** philosophy which guides one not to be upset with the problems instead take problem as a challenge and solve it energetically. The stories show that our problems are just man-made, therefore they have to be solved by man himself.

For ingesting the essence and feeling the insights of the tales, the author has given his narration and creative interpretation in the form of **'Fact Of The Matter'** and **'Popular Version'** in the modern context before and after **'Fact Unfolded'**. Thus the superficial way of reading this book is through wise understanding of the tales and their interpretation in the modern context to encounter and manage one's problems precisely. Gopal's stories are deep rooted in the realism of the prevalent Bengali life. Gopal was indeed a renowned entertainer whose countless stories where he outwits other fellow courtiers and men are mirth in **Bengal** and **Bangladesh** even to this day.

Modern education has led us to more literacy and less understanding. This book is designed to provide an all-round understanding for managing our problems. The morals from Gopal's tales have endurance without death and are beyond the reach of destruction.

So there is a need for all of us to immerse and nourish ourselves with the understanding as to how to manage our problems . . . . with this book as a small dose in the offing to start.

A really good read that shouldn't disappoint any reader. . . . .

Gopal Bhand's **P.R.O.B.L.E.M.** Philosophy for Success

'As weather shapes mountains, problems shape leaders.'

'Act with a commitment that every problem contains the ingredients of the solution within itself.'

'Problems are only opportunities in work clothes.'

This book is an assortment of many timeless stories of Gopal with thoughts, advice, anecdotes and hard-learned lessons on issues and themes related to day-to-day problems of life, which support such maxims. After a story is read, one is left with a fine thread of thought which slowly burrows deeper and one realises that Gopal was actually passing on a profound message to **'Manage the Problems'** neatly.

The stories guide one not to be upset with the problems, instead take problem as a challenge and solve it energetically. The stories show that our problems are just man-made, therefore they may be solved by man himself.

Gopal's stories empowers one to be successful and satisfied by interpreting **'PROBLEM'** as an acronym to signify essential, self-evident and universal qualities as follows:

Perceive the situation not to kill but strengthen us.

Resolve sternly to crush and overcome obstacles.

Opportunity lies on the face of the Obstacle itself.

Braving obstacles and hardships is nobler than retreat to tranquility.

Learn to unlock the door to opportunity.

Exert the body, heart and head to arrive at the solution.

Method ideally selected to solve the problem improves odd situations.

Not just that the stories are short instances that touch the reader's mind and heart but with the lessons and messages imparted by Gopal's stories, one should weed out anything that is superfluous in this tense and busy world to overcome the problems.

If one chews, digests and absorbs to use the rich wit and wisdom, one will understand that 'there are no problems in life, only opportunities' and would be able to *'Manage the Problems'* peacefully in life.

Stay Dumb

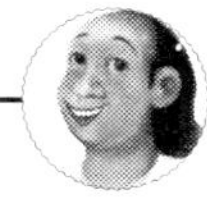

Fact of the Matter

Facts do not cease to exist because they are ignored. Hear one side, and you will be in the dark; hear both the sides, and all will be clear.

Fact Unfolded

Gopal as a young boy used to lazily roam around the whole town like a vagabond. He often visited the grocery shop of his neighbour Lakhindar who was quite showy and always boasted himself to be a brainy chap.

'Getting a Leg-up'

Once, Lakhindar pointing towards Gopal, whispered to an elderly customer, "You see, this is the dumbest kid in the world. Watch while I prove it to you."

Saying this, Lakhindar put a coin in one hand and a few *cowries*[1] in the other and called the boy to proudly ask, "Gopal, which one do you want, son?" Gopal smilingly took the *cowries* and left the shop. While Lakhindar and the customer both made fun of Gopal, he went to the nearest sweet shop to buy himself *sandesh*[2].

'What a dumb kid,' the customer continued to think for long. Later that day, the customer came across Gopal roaming lazily in the market place. Already puzzled by Gopal's peculiar behaviour noticed at Lakhindar's shop, the customer called Gopal and curiously asked, "Hey, son! May I ask you a question? Why did you take the *cowries* instead of the coin when you know that the coin has far more money value than the paltry *cowries*?"

Gopal with his mouthful of *sandesh* and smacking his lips replied, "It's simple! Because the day I take the coin, the game is over uncle!"

The customer blushed and walked away saying nothing.

Popular Version

Often one makes conclusions to his own disadvantage. A conclusion should never be a place where you got tired of thinking. Digging up facts may be a hard job, but it is much better than jumping at conclusions. To draw inferences, a wise man should proportion his belief to the evidence he has.

❁❁❁

1. *Cowrie (Kauri) is a glossy bright shell of any marine molluscs. It was used as money/currency in many parts of South Asia during ancient and medieval periods. It was the smallest unit of a coin in currency.*
2. *Sandesh is the heritage sweet dish/dessert of Bengal culture.*

Coming of Age

Fact of the Matter

Panchatantra rightly says, 'Learn from any who is wise, though a boy.'

Fact Unfolded

The 18th Century was a time of political chaos and instability in Bengal. The Mughal Empire was gradually declining after the death of *Aurangzeb*[1], and the Maratha Empire was rising.

In Bengal, the Muslim governors became independent, and the Nawabs were flourishing.

'Moment of Truth'

1. The last ruler (Sultan) of the Mughal Dynasty (Delhi Sultanate).

The Hindu Rajas were mostly semi-independent and had to depend on Nawabs for the Kingdoms' internal affairs. They had to face frequent torture because of Nawabs' indifferent approach towards non-Muslims, mainly the Hindus.

Once, a shrewd Nawab challenged the entire Krishnanagar Empire to answer his three peculiar questions. He proclaimed that the questions were a hard nut to crack and whosoever answers them would be undoubtedly acknowledged as a scholar.

No scholar in Krishnanagar could answer his three questions... thus he made fun of the Hindus publicly. He constantly ridiculed the Hindu population.

One day, the young vagabond Gopal heard the Nawab yelling and screaming at the innocent Hindus in the market place. He was challenging the people openly to answer his three questions.

Gopal stood quietly and watched. He decided to challenge the Nawab. He walked up and calmly told the Nawab, "I will accept your challenge."

The Nawab laughed at the boy and ridiculed the Hindus even more by saying, "A young lad of 16 summers challenges me. Is this all you have to offer!"

But Gopal patiently reiterated his stance. He continued to challenge the Nawab, and with *Maa Durga's*[2] help and guidance, he affirmed to put the Nawab's silly challenge to an end. The Nawab finally accepted Gopal's standpoint.

So, the next day, the entire city gathered around a small 'hillock' where open addresses were usually made. The Nawab climbed to

---

2. Hindu deity.

the top, and in a loud voice asked his first question, "You have great faith in your God! So tell me, what is your God doing right now?"

The young Gopal thought for a while and then told the Nawab to climb down the 'hillock' and allow him to go up in order to answer the question.

The Nawab said, "What? You want me to come down?"

Gopal said, "Yes. I need to reply, right?"

The Nawab made his way down and Gopal made his way up.

Gopal's replied, "Oh Almighty! You be my witness in front of all these people. You have just willed that a nasty, arrogant and cruel person be brought down to a low level, and that a holy, kind person of the masses be brought to a high level!"

The crowd cheered and screamed in excitement.

The Nawab was humiliated, but he boldly asked his second question ... "What existed before your God?"

Gopal thought and then he asked the Nawab softly, "Sire, please count from 10 backwards."

The Nawab started to count arrogantly... "10 . . 9 . . . 8 . . 7 . . 6 . . 5 . . 4 . . 3 . . 2 . . 1 . .0. ."

Gopal asked, "What comes before 0?" "...Nothing!" the Nawab declared with pride.

Gopal replied with his wandering eyes, "Exactly. Nothing existed before God, for He is eternal and absolute."

The crowd cheered again.... The people were thrilled and praised Gopal.

The Nawab, now completely frustrated, asked his final question harshly,"In which direction is your God facing?"

Gopal again thought and thought. He then asked for a candle. A candle was brought to him. Gopal handed it to the Nawab and asked him to light it.

The Nawab proudly did so and remarked,"What is this supposed to prove?"

The young Gopal politely asked, "In which direction is the light from the candle going?"

The Nawab responded,"It is going in all directions."

Gopal continued to explain in a clam and thoughtful manner, "You have answered your own question. God's light (aura) goes in all directions. He is everywhere. There is nowhere that He cannot be found."

The crowd cheered again....and overwhelmed with joy applauded Gopal.

The Nawab stood speechless. He was so impressed and moved with young Gopal's knowledge and spirituality that he hugged Gopal and swore never to ridicule the people or their religious sentiments.

So ended the never-ending debate.

Popular Version

Wisdom is the power to put our time, awareness and knowledge to proper use at an opportunate moment for converting unfavourable circumstances into favourable ones. This is the evolution, less and less in the body and more and more in the mind.

Masterstrokes

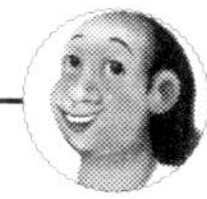

Fact of the Matter

For life to turn into a great victory, you have to win many small battles along the way.

Fact Unfolded

Gopal Bhand had lost both his parents when he was still quite young. He lived all by himself in the village. He just had a goat with which he stayed in a tiny thatched hut.

Gopal had two mischievous uncles, who always tried to cheat him out of his goat and hut. They made his life really miserable.

One day, the uncles stole his goat and tied it alongside some other goats that belonged to the village butcher. Poor Gopal looked everywhere for it. The butcher, meanwhile, took all the goats and killed them for their meat. Now, Gopal's goat wore a distinct bell around its neck. When the butcher cut that goat, he threw away the bell. Gopal found the bell soon after and was heartbroken. He knocked at the butcher's door for justice. By then the butcher had realised that he had killed Gopal's goat and felt sorry. Scared that the boy would tell everyone he had killed a stolen goat, the butcher anyhow gave Gopal some money and sent him away.

When the uncles saw their nephew coming home with the coins

tinkling in his pocket, they were amazed. How had Gopal made money from a lost goat? When they asked, Gopal said, "Everyone wanted goat's meat today in the market. My poor goat somehow ended up at the butcher's shop. He sold its meat and made a lot of money. This is my share."

The uncles thought this was a good way to make money. The next day, they bought fifty goats and slaughtered all of them and went to the market to sell the meat. But now there was so much meat in the market that the prices had come down and they got only few coins for their goats. So they incurred heavy loss.

Angry at being fooled, they decided to burn down Gopal's hut. So one night, when Gopal had gone out, they set fire to his little hut. The young boy was stunned to come home and find a pile of blazing ash where his hut used to be. At once he knew who was behind it. Miserably, he gathered the ash in a bag and decided to leave the village forever. With the bag slung over his shoulder, he set off. After walking for many miles, he at last reached a village near Kutabpur. He sat down under a tree to rest and thought what to do next.

He sat under the tree all day long. The passing villagers watched Gopal sitting under the tree. Soon a crowd of curious villagers gathered around him. 'Who was this stranger? Why was he carrying a bag of ashes,' they all wondered. Finally one man asked him, "What is the matter? Why are you sitting quietly like this? Why are you carrying so much ash with you?"

Gopal's hut had been his dearest, most blessed possession, so he said, "It is the ash from a holy place."

Now the villagers were eager. "Will you sell it to us?" they asked. "No," replied Gopal.

But the desperate villagers did not gave up. "Give us a pinch at least," they begged. Gopal agreed and gave them a pinch of ash each. Soon, word spread in the village that, 'a holy man had come from the *Hindu Kush*[1], who looked like he was in his twenties but was really more than seventy years old. He was carrying a bag of sacred ashes with him that could cure all hardships, misfortunes and disease. He was giving away a pinch of it to each person, and though he wanted no money, it was only right that you paid him a coin at least for such happiness.'

Thus a long queue formed in front of Gopal. Each villager took a pinch of ash and left a coin in return. At the end of the day, Gopal discovered that the ash was all gone and in its place he had a heap of coins.

'Going For the Chase'

---

1. *Sub-mountainous range of the grand Himalayas.*

Cheerfully, he decided to go back to his village and start life afresh. When he came back, his uncles could not believe their eyes. How had Gopal done this? They asked Gopal his secret. Gopal said, "There is a great demand for ashes in that village near Kutabpur. I sold the ash that I gathered from my burnt hut and got all this money."

Both the uncles were amazed. If Gopal could get so much money by selling the ash from his little hut, how much would they get if they burnt their grand houses and sold the ash? That night itself, they burnt down their houses, gathered the ashes in huge sacks and set off for the village near Kutabpur. But as soon as they reached and uttered the word 'ash', all the villagers pounced on them and beat them battered and tattered! By then the villagers knew there was nothing magical in the ash. And here were two more people trying to fool them!

The uncles somehow saved their skins and ran home. Now they were even angrier with Gopal for having deceived them a second time. They decided to kill him. One day, they invited him for a walk with them by the River Bhagirathi. As they stood on the bridge, where the river was at its deepest, one of them pointed at the water and exclaimed, "See! A gorgeous *mermaid*[2]!"

As soon as Gopal leaned over to look in the water, they pushed him from behind and ran home. Poor Gopal nearly drowned. Just in time, a girl washing clothes nearby heard his screams for help and dived in. She was a good swimmer and saved his life.

A grateful Gopal told her the story of his life. The girl felt pity at Gopal. She thought for a while and then whispered a plan in his ear.

---

2. *A mermaid is a mythical sea creature with a head and upper body of a woman and the tail of a fish instead of legs.*

The next day Gopal arrived at his uncles' house. With him was the girl, dressed in beautiful clothes and jewellery. Gopal also held a fine bag in his hands. His uncles were astonished to see him alive. How had he survived? Gopal said,"When I fell into the river, this fine-looking girl saved me. She has a Palace at the bottom of the river. She fell in love with me and married me. She also gave me half her riches. Now we will live in the river. Do come and visit us some time." Saying this, they left in the direction of the river. The uncles had a quick discussion and decided that they would follow Gopal to his Palace in the river and perhaps cheat him of his latest riches. So they hurriedly ran to the river and dived into its deep waters.

They were never heard of again.

Popular Version

You can let a bad situation overwhelm and embitter you, or you can decide what must be done, do it, and get on with your life.

Be a remarkable, un-duplicatable, and miraculous leader who does what has to be done when it needs to be done, regardless of the consequences. That maturity has more to do with what types of experiences you've had and what you've learnt from them, and less to do with how many birthdays you've celebrated. When you are playing against other card players, good or bad, you don't tell them anything about what is there in your hand. In fact, you may even smile and look confident when you have a bad or mediocre hand. You know that your confident look may encourage your competitor to pull back. On the other hand, you may show disgust when you have a good hand. This encourages the competitor to stay in. This was exactly what Gopal did with his cunning uncles. So, put all your energy into your game, and read your rival to conquer.

Star Power

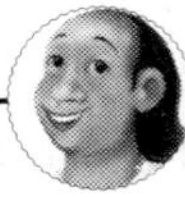

Fact of the Matter

When coping with difficult situations, our first step should be to think straight and react with our mind rather than our emotions. This is often easier said than done.

Fact Unfolded

Gopal Bhand and his childhood friend Subrata were quick and bright in the entire village. Both were good in responding to situations and usually competed with each other in the practice of it.

'Leading From the Front'

Once, they decided to find out which of them was cleverer in his art. Subrata said that he could rob the eggs of a bird while it was hatching them in its nest on the top of a tree. Gopal listened to Subrata's challenge and said, "That's really a tough job. Anyway prove yourself and go ahead. I will do my trick afterwards."

They went to a tall tree on the top of which was a nest. In it sat a bird, hatching. Subrata stealthily crawled up the tree, stole two eggs and came down. In great happiness, he told Gopal that he had done it. Gopal asked Subrata to show the eggs he had stolen. Subrata put his hand in his pocket. But lo. . . . he found that there was only one egg, the other was just a dead stone. He was puzzled.

Gopal laughed at him and produced the missing egg from his pocket. Gopal said, "You thought that you have stolen two eggs from the nest; but I had already stolen one from the nest and put the stone there instead."

Both laughed heartily. There was no need for Gopal to prove his better talents to Subrata.

Popular Version

Some people can't bear to have anything go wrong or be unfinished. We call them perfectionists. In their particular vision of the world, there is no room for anything but perfection. This view persists regardless of how difficult the task or the volume of work.

What an Idea!

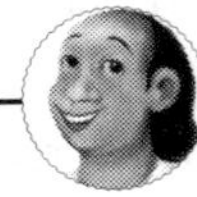

Fact of the Matter

What the caterpillar calls the end of the world, the master calls a butterfly.

Fact Unfolded

The young Gopal had a rich friend named Sarat who always boasted of his wealth. When Gopal asked Sarat about his riches, he used to explain, "You can also become rich like me. You just have to try your luck in *Bulandshahr*, *Hastinapur* or *Indraprastha*[1]. These are lucrative business places and full of opportunities."

'Mesh of Creativity'

---

1. Prosperous business cities of those times. Nowadays located in Northern India.

Gopal was fully impressed with Sarat's words. One day, he decided to go to distant lands for business. To tell about his plans and seek advice, Gopal went to his ailing father who was a man of learning. He became happy with Gopal's decision and gave him some advice, "Gopal. . . You are a simple village lad. When you do business and travel to foreign lands, make sure you know the local culture well. Try to gain as much information as you can before you go there. Only your knowledge and presence of mind will come to your help in an unknown land."

Gopal listened to his father's words carefully. Next day, he left for a faraway country for business. There, he stayed in an Inn. He got talking to its owner and, without realising, ended up telling the man all about his life, business plans and his father.

Next day, he went to the market, and was amazed when a one-armed man rushed to him and said, "Your father took one of my arms as a loan. You must return it to me." Not knowing what to do, Gopal asked for a day to think about this. Then, a woman came to him and said, "Your father married me. He used to send me money every month. Now that he has fled from here, you must give me money." Again Gopal asked for a day's relief and walked away. He stopped at another Inn and had a meal. When he went to make his payment, the owner said, "I only want you to make me happy." Though he had to pay only one coin, Gopal gave the man two, but still he said he was unhappy. Puzzled, Gopal walked away.

Later that day, a man invited him to play *Chausar*[2]. Poor Gopal did not know that they were playing the game with a trick dice. He lost all the games. But the man who won set an unusual condition,

---

2. *Chausar, Chaupar or Chaupad is a skilful, complex and older game of dice.*

"You must drink all the water in the sea, or else give me all the goods you have brought here to sell." Poor Gopal again said that he would be back the next day with his answer.

Gopal was baffled with the city's shocking behaviour. That night, as he lay in his bed, he remembered his father's words, 'In a foreign land only your wits will come to your aid.'

The next morning, as soon as he went to the market, the one-armed man appeared before him. Gopal greeted him with a big smile and said, "You were right. My father took many hands like yours and our house is full of hands. Give me your other hand. I will find the matching one and send it to you." The man ran away in fright.

Then he found the woman who claimed to have been married to his father, "Mother!" he shouted, "My father was wrong not to have told me about you. Now you are like a second mother to me. My father is now old and weak. Come home with me and help my mother in the fields." The woman too made a quick getaway when she heard this.

Next he went to the hotel. The owner was standing outside. Gopal shouted to him, "Hail the King! Your King is the best in the world!" the man had no choice but to answer, "You are right. I am very happy that you think so."

"If you are happy, I have paid for my meal," said Gopal and went to find the man with the game of *Chausar*. When he found him, he said, "I have thought over the challenge. I will drink all the water in the sea. But you have to bring me the water in jugs." That man too ran away when he heard this.

Gopal went on to do business in that country but soon decided to leave the country due to more wicked people he encountered each day.

Popular Version

Life is more than just a word. Each day comes as a new adventure, a new challenge, and a new quest, which has to be tackled with sharpness, awareness and alertness. Seekers respond to this simple wisdom.

Warning Signs

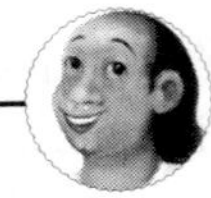

Fact of the Matter

Set a thief to catch a thief.

Fact Unfolded

Gopal was poor and stayed in a shanty (hutment) near a *dighi*[1] in the outskirts of Krishnanagar. His envious neighbour Kushad had an evil eye on the land where Gopal's hut stood.

'Summative Assessments'

1. *Water Patch*

So, Gopal Bhand was once taken to the *Adhikari*[2] by Kushad who claimed that he owned the land on which Gopal's hut stood.

Gopal had sufficient testimony to prove that he owned the land but he knew that the *Adhikari* who was to decide the dispute was immensely corrupt and could be bought. So Gopal decided to take a gift for the *Adhikari*.

At the hearing, Kushad stated his case and then taking out a fat purse from one of his pockets transferred it to another in a slow and deliberate manner. The *Adhikari* understood. He looked at Gopal as if to ask him if he could match the offer.

In answer, Gopal patted his own pocket. The *Adhikari* was pleased to see that Gopal's pocket was bulging. He could make out the outlines of two large objects in it and he felt sure they were nothing else than gold ornaments.

He gave a verdict in Gopal's favour and called him to his chamber. Gopal went round to the Adhikari's chamber and began to thank him for deciding the case in his favour. But the *Adhikari* cut him short with an impatient gesture of his hand. "The gift," he snapped. "Give me whatever you have brought for me!"

Gopal smilingly took out two large stones from his pocket and gave them to the *Adhikari*. The *Adhikari* had nothing to say but stood staggered. Gopal slowly moved out of the chamber contended.

Popular Version

Nothing contributes more than method. A dishonest person can only be tackled with trick.

❁❁❁

2. *Official deputed by the State to accomplish defined purposes relating to revenue, tax, law and order and so on.*

Tough Opponent

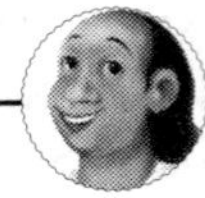

Fact of the Matter

A fair exchange of excuses is no robbery.

Fact Unfolded

In a small village on the outskirts of Krishnanagar, the *Zamindaar* decided to build a rest house with a *dighi*[1] for the wandering *sadhus*[2] and *sanyasis*[3]. He invited, or rather, commanded the men of the village over whom he held influence, to work on the project.

"You will earn merit by this work and attain *moksha*[4]. You will be relieved of your sins," he announced. "So I will not pay you!"

The miserly *Zamindaar* was habitual of not paying the people for their work and everybody understood his lame excuses, but nobody wanted to displease him. So all the able-bodied men of the village came to help. All, except the village simpleton Gopal, marvelled to perform. But Gopal just sat lazily on a log and watched the others work.

The *Zamindaar's* blood boiled when he spotted the idler. "Why aren't you working!" he screamed.

---

1. *Water patch.*
2. *Holy wandering hermits.*
3. *Salvation/liberation.*
4. *Zamindaars were an aristocratic and typically hereditary class who lived during pre-Independent India and held enormous tracts of land.*

"I would have liked to work on this noble undertaking," said Gopal innocently, rising to his feet, "but my stomach is empty. Who can work on an empty stomach?"

Seeing that Gopal was healthy and full-bodied and capable of contributing massively to the task on hand, the *Zamindaar* ordered his servants to feed him. This took a long time as Gopal kept on asking for second and third servings of food that was being provided to him. But finally he pushed his plate aside, belched loudly and went to wash.

Then Gopal returned to the site.

Sometime later the *Zamindaar* went to inspect the work and was furious to see Gopal again sitting idly on the log.

"Why aren't you working!" he roared.

"I would have liked to work," said Gopal, rising to his feet. "Indeed I want to work on this noble undertaking. But my stomach is full. Who can work on a full stomach?"

The *Zamindaar* did not say anything but felt thunderstruck at Gopal's reply.

Popular Version

A worst excuse should be countered by a rational exchange of a terrible excuse.

Speaking his Mind

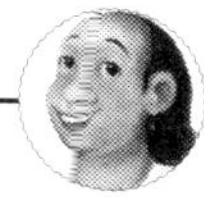

Fact of the Matter

One has to see an opportunity in a difficulty rather than seeing difficulty in an opportunity.

Fact Unfolded

Before becoming a court jester, Gopal Bhand owned a small piece of land in *Birnagar*[1] and did farming on it for a livelihood. The *Zamindaar*[2] was a cruel and greedy person and brother of the local *Nawab*[3].

'Great Going'

1. *Birnagar is a big town close to Krishnanagar in Nadia District in the State of West Bengal.*
2. *Zamindaar was an aristocrat, typically hereditary, who held enormous tracts of land and ruled over and taxed the peasants who lived on it during the pre-Independence period.*
3. *Nawab is an honorific title given to male Muslim rulers of princely Indian States. It is the Muslim equivalent of the term Maharaja that was granted to Hindu rulers. The title of Nawab was also awarded as a personal distinction to persons and families who never ruled a princely state.*

One day the *Zamindaar* came to see Gopal who was working profusely in his field.

"These fields belonged to my father's father," said the *Zamindaar*. "I will take half of whatever you grow in these fields," the *Zamindaar* said to Gopal commandingly.

Gopal was frightened but he kept his wits about him.

"You can take whatever grows above the ground, Your Excellency," Gopal said without any resistance. The *Zamindaar* agreed and went away.

That year Gopal grew potatoes in his field. When the *Zamindaar* came for his share, he only got the stems and leaves of the plant but since they grew underground, not a single potato.

"Next time I'll take whatever grows below the ground!" the *Zamindaar* growled in anger.

When he came again some months later, Gopal was harvesting corn. He had planted corn and had got a bumper harvest. "Where's my share!" screamed the Zamindaar.

"Your share is under the ground, Your Excellency," said Gopal, "You can take the roots away whenever you want."

The *Zamindaar* felt ashamed at being outwitted by Gopal, turned around without another word and walked away.

A few months later, the cruel *Zamindaar* imposed a heavy tax on agricultural produce.

That year, *Birnagar* faced a severe drought and the crops failed miserably.

Gopal went to the *Zamindaar* and begged to exempt him from payment of tax, "My land is not doing too well and I have a large family to support. I beg My Lord to exempt me from the payment of tax," Gopal explained.

"That does not concern me," said the *Zamindaar*, "pay the tax or leave the town."

"Where will I go?" said Gopal in a distraught voice.

"Go to Karimpur or Gayespur," said the *Zamindaar*, "they are prosperous towns."

"That is true," said Gopal seriously. "But your nephew rules Karimpur and he has made the same laws, and as for Gayespur, it is ruled by your cousin."

"Then go to the *Nawab* and complain," said the *Zamindaar*, impatiently.

"The *Nawab* is your brother," continued Gopal. "He will not accept my request."

"Then go to Hell!" roared the *Zamindaar*.

"Ah, yes, Hell! That would be fine," said Gopal, gravely. "But pardon me, Your Excellency, did not your respected father die last year?"

The *Zamindaar* though cruel had a sense of humour. He laughed at Gopal's quick wit and agreed to exempt Gopal from the tax.

Popular Version

Instead of solving the problem, we often create a philosophy as to why a problem should not exist and thus struggle to prove that philosophy to be right. This attitude creates inner prisons. Instead we should understand as to what is the prime requirement. The answer is that we should all have addictive habits to go for solving the problem(s) whenever and wherever encountered.

More on
The Anvil

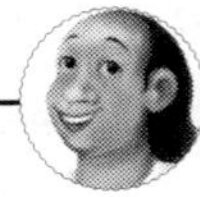

Fact of the Matter

Should we dig a hole and live in it throughout our lives? Or should we endeavour to turn adversity into advantage through understanding and effort?

Fact Unfolded

Before becoming a court jester in the *Rajbari*[1], the jobless and homeless Gopal decided to seek his luck in the pious city of Nabadwip.

'Sheer Exhilaration meets total control'

1. *The Royal Court/Palace*

The first thing he did in Nabadwip was of course to visit the *Sonar Gouranga Mandiram*[2]. There, he prayed earnestly asking God to help him find a livelihood.

One day, after finishing his prayers, when Gopal was just passing through the temple corridor, a proud and haughty priest asked him the way to the village pond. Gopal explained him the route patiently for which the priest thanked him saying, "You seem to be a bright and courteous man. Would you like to listen to my sermon this evening so that I may show you the way to Heaven?"

"You're going to show me the way to heaven," Gopal asked the priest surprisingly, "when you don't even know the way to the village pond." Hearing this, the priest stood dumbstruck.

At this, the temple's old caretaker witnessing Gopal's unexpected wit got impressed and approached him to explain, "I see you here every day praying sincerely before God. You seem to be from outside this city... Is there anything which I can do to help you?"

"Indeed," replied Gopal, "I left my home in search of a job."

"You appear to be mature beyond your years. Rather, you are old head on young shoulders. Would you consider being an assistant to the *Archaka*[3] of this *Mandiram*?" said the caretaker curiously. Gopal immediately accepted the offer happily.

---

2. *Nabadwip is one of the most prominent pilgrimage destinations for Vaishnavas because it was here that Shri Chaitanya Mahaprabhu, the founder of Vaishnav religion and great social reformer were born and spent considerable period of his lifetime. The Sonar Gouranga Mandiram is one of the most famous temples in Nabadwip. The temple has the Golden Shrine of Shri Chaitanya Mahaprabhu. His footwear has been kept here, in a glass case.*
3. *Archaka means Pujari i.e. Priest who does Puja (worship or religious ritual performed by Hindus as an offering to various deities) in Mandiram (Hindu temple). Pujaris learn and chant vedic manthras.*

As a ritual, on every Tuesday, the temple had an auspicious congregation of people where the *Archaka* had to deliver a holy sermon and recite *mantras*[4]. The *Archaka* was renowned all over the city for his Tuesdays' sermons.

So, as usual, on a Tuesday, people flocked the *Mandiram* in large numbers for the *Archaka's* sermon.

Unfortunately, just before the sermon, the *Archaka* had to urgently leave the temple. He had to visit distant Devagram town to attend his ailing mother. Before leaving, the *Archaka* advised Gopal to handle the devotees with care.

Though he was experiencing the sermons for the last few weeks, but Gopal knew nothing about the scriptures. He was perplexed as how to deal with the odd situation and counter the people. However, Gopal gathered courage to approach the stage and said, "My dear brothers. Do you have any idea what the sermon would be on this Tuesday?" The congregation all responded, "No!" "If you don't know, then why are you here? Go home," replied Gopal.... and they all left mutely.

The following Tuesday, the congregation again gathered. The *Archaka* had not returned yet. Poor Gopal had to again counter the odd situation. Anyhow, he approached the stage and said, "My dear brothers. Do you know what my sermon is for you this Tuesday?" All responded, "Yes!" "If you already know, then what are you doing here? Go home". . . . and they all again left speechless.

The following Tuesday, still the *Archaka* had not returned. Gopal

---

4. *Sacred hymns, texts, verses ('aartis') or vedic scriptures or itihaasas (histories in epic) of Hindu religion predominantly composed in Sanskrit and dedicated to God.*

again had to counter the devotees. He approached the pulpit (stage) and said, "My, dear brothers. Have you any idea what our sermon would be this Tuesday?" The crowd had agreed previously that if Gopal repeat this question again, they would confuse him. Half of the devotees said "Yes!" and half said "No!" Gopal thought for a while and gently replied, "Well the group that knows, please tell those who don't know ... My brothers!!!" and saying this he quietly left the pulpit leaving the people more astonished than before.

Gopal smiled to himself on the manner he tackled the odd situation. This was how Gopal Bhand countered the people with his wit.

Popular Version

Now call this a small dishonesty, or a big one – it is all about how we want to make ourselves feel! We all have ways of making ourselves feel good. So, yes of course, these are all small lies. But, are they really good? Why then do we need to tell ourselves yet another lie in order to feel better?

Aiming for Reform

Fact of the Matter

A crocodile remains a crocodile even if dressed in silk.

Fact Unfolded

Gopal Bhand and his wife was a poor old couple having a buffalo as their precious procession. Once, Gopal fell seriously sick due to malaria. Soon all their money was consumed in buying medicines for Gopal. So they were left with no option but to sell their dear buffalo. Gopal's wife would have to go to the market to sell the buffalo. She was a simple lady, so Gopal strictly warned her, "You know this city is

'Quartet of Errors'

full of *thugs*[1], so don't talk to anyone on your way. Just walk straight to the market, sell the buffalo and come back with the money safely."

The next morning, the lady headed towards the market, leading the buffalo by a thick rope. On the way, she met three young men. They were the local *thugs* and enjoyed harassing helpless and poor people. When they saw the lady with her buffalo, they decided to play a trick. One of them tip-toed behind her, freed the buffalo and tied a donkey in its place. The lady had just been walking engrossed in deep thought, worried about the ailing Gopal. So she did not notice the trick. But soon, she was stunned to hear a donkey braying behind her. When she looked back she found that her buffalo had vanished and she was holding just a donkey!

The three *thugs* came up to her and said, "There is magic in the air and magic everywhere. It turned your buffalo into a donkey."

The poor lady walked on with the donkey. After a while, the *thugs* secretly freed the donkey to tie a fowl in its place, 'Cockooo. . . . . .,' crowed the fowl and the lady was amazed again. Now the donkey had become a fowl!

The three *thugs* again screamed, "Magic in the air and magic everywhere, Auntie."

The lady now walked on with the fowl. The thugs stealthily crept up again and tied a wooden block in place of the fowl. The lady was surprised to hear the sound of wood dragging on the road behind her. "Magic in the air and magic everywhere, Auntie," shouted the *thugs* again.

Then as she dragged the wood helplessly, the *thugs* untied the piece of wood too and ran away. When the lady reached the market,

---

1. *Members of a well-organized grouping of professional cheats.*

she found that she was just holding a rope in her hand. Feeling sad, she came back home. She had lost the buffalo and not got any money either. When she told Gopal about the sad story of the magic, he understood what had happened. He told his wife,"Tomorrow make *Cholar Dal*, *Khichuri*, *Luchi* and *Payesh*[2] for lunch. Make sure you cook for three people. I will come home with some guests. As soon as they come, you must obediently say,'I have cooked what the rabbit told me. Come eat your lunch.' Rest leave everything else to me."

The next morning, the weak and ill Gopal gathered some energy, went straight to his friend and borrowed two identical rabbits from him. He left one at home and tied the other with a string and started walking towards the market with it. On the way, he too met the three thugs. "Hey, Uncle!" they shouted, "Your wife's buffalo vanished yesterday. Where are you taking this rabbit now?"

Gopal looked unhappily at the thugs and said,"This rabbit is just like my son. It obeys my every word. But now I am sick and need money, so I am going to sell it today in the market."

The three *thugs* were surprised when they heard this, "Does it really understand what you say, Uncle?" they asked surprisingly.

"Of course it does. Here, watch me." Gopal turned to the rabbit and said,"My son .... Jump home and tell your mother to make *Cholar Dal*, *Khichuri*, *Luchi* and *Payesh* for three people."Then he untied the string and let the rabbit hop away. Then he said to the *thugs*,"Come home and have lunch with me today."

When all reached Gopal's house, his wife welcomed them and said,"I have cooked what the rabbit told me. Come, eat your lunch."

---

2. *Cholar Dal is Bengal gram cooked with coconut; Khichuri is a simple Bengali rice recipe; Luchi is Bengali roti made by deep frying flour discs; and Payesh is rice pudding.*

And she laid out *Cholar Dal*, *Khichuri*, *Luchi* and *Payesh* for each of them. What was more; they saw the rabbit sitting in a corner of the room tucking into a carrot!

They were surprised to see all this and told Gopal, "We will buy your rabbit."

Gopal pretended to think for a while and then said, "My boys, it is very precious to me. How can I sell it?" When the three begged him and offered more and more money, he reluctantly agreed. They dropped a heap of coins in his hand and rushed away with the rabbit.

Now, the *thugs* had been blackmailing the *taluqdar*[3] for some money. They said to the rabbit, "Go tell the taluqdar to come and give us our money within ten minutes or face the consequences."

The rabbit hopped off and the thugs waited for the *taluqdar*. An hour went by, but there was no sign of either the *taluqdar* or the rabbit. They marched straight to his house, knocked loudly on the door and demanded, "Give us our money and the rabbit."

The furious *taluqdar* ordered his toughest guard to give them a sound thrashing.

Bleeding and battered black and blue, the three *thugs* went back to Gopal, "You fooled us!" they shouted, "Give us back our money at once."

"There is magic in the air and magic everywhere," sighed Gopal, "The money has disappeared my boys!"

Hearing these words, the *thugs* ran away to be never seen again.

---

3. Indian land holders during Mughal and British times, responsible for maintaining law & order besides collecting taxes from the province(s).

Popular Version

Fight against set notions, superstitions, falsehood, limitations, and most importantly against 'UNFAIRNESS' is essential. Unfairness is a part and parcel of life. He that cheats shall be cheated. Such should be the way of life. And Gopal Bhand practiced it profoundly.

Mental Issues

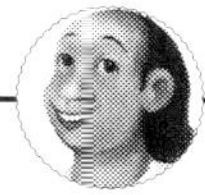

Fact of the Matter

Never complain. Every situation will teach you something. If you succeed, it is good; if not, you learn what not to do!

Fact Unfolded

Gopal Bhand, the poor barber lived with his wife in Krishnanagar. To supplement his scanty earnings, Gopal used to till a field that belonged to the *Zamindaar*.

Gopal and his wife loved each other dearly, and were happy together. But Gopal's wife had one fault. She was a big chatterbox,

'Prescription for Gains'

who didn't know when to hold her tongue. Anything her husband told her would be all over the village the following day!

One day Gopal was working in the field when his plough struck something hard and metallic. Curious, he took his spade and began digging at the spot. Soon, he uncovered a large chest. He opened it and discovered — to his great joy — that it was full of gold coins!

He thought, 'This treasure must have been buried by the original owner of the land, generations ago. Since then, the land has changed hands several times. Our *Zamindaar* bought it only a couple of years ago. So I have as good a right to the money as anyone else!'

But how was he to take the money home? Gopal's house was far off from the field and if someone saw the big chest on the way, it would cause grave problems. The matter would reach the *Zamindaar's* ears and he would seize the treasure. So Gopal decided to leave the chest in the field for the time being. After taking out a heap of gold coins, he buried the chest securely again. He took the coins home in a bag.

Knowing his wife's nature, Gopal decided, 'It's best that my wife know nothing about it for the present. If she comes to know, she won't be able to resist telling the neighbours, and before I know it, the *Zamindaar* will hear the news! So I'd better keep it a secret, and tell her after I've had a chance to hide the money!'

Unfortunately for Gopal, his wife saw him entering the house with a bag containing gold coins. She asked Gopal what the bag contained and where he had got it from? Gopal was left with no choice but to tell her the truth. He concluded with the warning to her, "Remember, you must not breathe a word about this to anybody, or there'll be a great trouble for both of us!"

"What do you take for me?" asked his wife angrily. "Of course I won't tell anyone. Anyone at all!" she assured Gopal.

Well, she did mean to keep the secret, and perhaps she would have too, if her best friend, Kunshi, hadn't happened to drop in immediately after Gopal left! When Kunshi asked her why she looked so exited, Gopal's wife, unable to restrain herself, burst out, "Oh, Kunshi, it's wonderful news! My husband has found a fabulous treasure in his field! But you're not to tell anyone of this, it's a secret!" warned Gopal's wife.

"Of course you can rely on me to keep the secret!" promised Kunshi. But all the same she could not resist repeating the story to just one another person – her sister-in-law, the carpenter's wife. She in turn told the weaver's wife, who in turn told the cobbler's wife and so on, until just two hours later, the news of Gopal's find had reached the ears of the *Zamindaar* himself.

The *Zamindaar* decided to check out the matter for himself, and immediately rode out to Gopal's house, which lay far out at a lonely open area. Gopal's wife was alone there. The *Zamindaar* asked her, "Listen... .woman, is it true that your husband has found a treasure on my land?"

Trembling with fear, Gopal's wife stammered, "It's .... it's true Sire!"

"Well then, where is Gopal?" demanded the *Zamindaar*.

She replied that Gopal had gone out. The *Zamindaar* asked where the treasure was, and she answered truthfully that she did not know where Gopal had hidden it. Nor did she know where Gopal had gone, or when he would be back.

Finally, the *Zamindaar* furiously declared, "I'm going out on a journey tomorrow and will be away for a few days. But depend on it,

I'll get to the bottom of this as soon as I return!" He then rode away.

When Gopal returned home, his wife told him all that had happened during his absence. He did not say anything to her, but started to think quickly about his future course of action.

Soon, he had an idea and smiled to himself as he thought of it.

Near their house was a deep forest with a stream flowing through it. Gopal bought several large *hilsha*[2] and a bagful of *Luchi*, *Sandesh* and Jhal *Muri*[3]. He entered the forest and climbed a tree. He carefully tied a fish to one of its branches in such a way that from below, it appeared that the fish was sitting on the branch. He attached the remaining fish to other branches. Then he scattered the snacks – *Luchi*, *Sandesh* and *Jhal Muri* on the tops of bushes and trees. As the forest was usually deserted, he was sure that no one would come to disturb his arrangements.

All his preparations done, Gopal returned home and asked his wife to accompany him to the nearby town of Vishnupur. She readily agreed. They set off in their little horse-cart. Gopal deliberately avoided the path through the forest.

On reaching the town, Gopal exchanged some of the gold coins he had brought for groceries and house hold articles. The couple then began their return journey. By then the sun had set, and it was growing dark.

They had reached the outskirts of Krishnanagar when Gopal, who was driving the cart, looked upwards towards the sky and remarked, "It looks as if there's been a big storm! I think we'd better take the short cut through the forest, so that we get home quickly!"

---

2. A popular oily and tropical fish.

3. Luchi is Bengali roti made by deep frying flour discs; Sandesh is Bengali Sweet dish and Jhal Muri is a tea time Bengali snack.

"Yes, yes, do that!" the lady agreed unresistingly.

As they were driving through the forest, Gopal suddenly stopped the cart with a jerk, exclaiming, "Gracious! If that isn't the strangest thing I've ever seen!"

"What's the matter, Gopal?" Gopal's wife asked in surprise.

"Just look at that!" said Gopal to his wife, pointing to a tree. "Bless my soul, if those aren't fish up there on that tree!"

She gaped at the tree, unable to believe her eyes. "But how on earth could the fish get up a tree?" she demanded at last.

"Well," said Gopal, pretending to be lost in thought, "There's only one explanation to this. The vibrations of the storm must have caused the fish to come out of the stream and climb the tree!"

"Good heaven! What a storm it must have been!" shuddered his wife.

"Anyway, I'll gather all these fish, so that we can cook them for dinner!" said Gopal and he quickly climbed a tree. He was busy gathering the fish one after the other, when a sudden scream from his wife stopped him short.

"Gopal! Look! There are sweets and snacks – *Sandesh*, *Luchi* and *Jhal Muri* all over the ground and on the bushes and trees too!" she cried in wonder. "Good, tasty snacks! Where on earth did they come from?" She picked up the sweets and snacks at top speed as she spoke.

"My goodness!" exclaimed Gopal, pretending to be very surprised. "Don't tell me it's rained *Sandesh*, *Luchi* and *Jhal Muri* during the storm!"

"It must be so," she said wonderstruck. "This sure beats everything I've seen. It is a night of marvels, indeed!"

Having gathered up the fish and the snacks, the couple resumed their journey. They came out of the forest and entered the city. As they were passing the *Zamindaar's* residence on their way, the loud braying of a donkey broke the silence.

"Good heavens! What's that ghostly noise?" she asked startled.

Gopal thought quickly. "I've heard that our *Zamindaar* had borrowed some money from the devil. As he did not pay the interest on time, the devil appears at night now and then and whips the *Zamindaar*. The sound we just heard is that of the devil torturing our *Zamindaar*!"

"Oh my goodness!" she cried in horror. Let's get out of here as quickly as possible!" Grinning, Gopal pulled the reins and they were off at a gallop. Soon they were home, and had no further adventures that night.

Two days later, the *Zamindaar* rode out to Gopal's house and found him standing outside. "Where's the treasure you found on my land?" he demanded.

"What treasure, Sire?" asked Gopal in mock surprise, "I know nothing of any treasure!"

"Don't try to play the fool with me!" warned the *Zamindaar* sternly. "It will do you no good to deny it. Your wife herself told me all about your finding the treasure!"

"Dear Sire! You don't mean to tell me that you have ridden all this way believing what she told you?" exclaimed Gopal. "Don't you know Sire that my poor wife is not quite sensible? The things she says sometimes are not really true."

"It's no use trying to bluff me, Gopal!" said the *Zamindaar*. "Call your wife here at once!"

Gopal called his wife.

"Didn't you tell me your husband found a chest full of gold coins in my field?" the *Zamindaar* demanded.

"Yes, Sire," she replied, "and I was with him in Vishnupur when he exchanged the gold coins for groceries and household articles!"

"When was this?" the *Zamindaar* asked next.

"It was the day of that terrible storm, when we found the fish up the tree," she relied promptly.

The *Zamindaar* stared at her, unable to believe his ears.

"Yes, Sire! The storm had driven them up there," she replied. "And what a storm it was, raining so many sweets and snacks – *Sandesh*, *Luchi* and *Jhal Muri*!"

The *Zamindaar* now began to suspect that Gopal was right about his wife's sense after all. He looked at Gopal, who smiled and tapped the side of his head sympathetically.

The *Zamindaar* turned back to the lady, "A storm that rained sweets and snacks, you say? When did this happen?" he asked.

"Well, Sire, it was the same evening that the devil whipped you for not paying his dues!"

"What nonsense!" shouted the *Zamindaar*, losing his temper, "Get out of my sight at once!" the lady rushed indoors in fright.

"Your wife is just a crazy and insensible creature. She is a mad lady!" the *Zamindaar* barked, turning to Gopal. He mounted his horse and rode off again leaving Gopal grinning from ear to ear.

Gopal was happy with his wit and enjoyed the treasure to live happily with his wife.

A repetitive mind is a psychological prison. 'Creativity' alone can release the 'Ability' from the prison of' 'Repetitive Thinking'.

Popular Version

Well, what is it that blocks creativity? One main enemy that blocks imaginative thinking is a 'repetitive mind'. If we think with a repetitive mind, we can't find any solution to our problems. This is what prevents us from viewing any issue from a totally new perspective. So rather being an oxen-bound-at-the-oil-mill, and victim of repetitive mind, be a victor of the situation. Be creative is to respect the creator in ourselves. Exercising our creativity often entails struggle, but the result is joy and an expanded sense of possibility. It requires us to go beyond the known, the familiar; it is the urge to explore new ground, a willingness to step outside our comfort zone. By bringing out our creative capacities, we can begin to surmount and transform the challenges that confront us.

Good Luck, Dear Gopal

Fact of the Matter

'When God gives us problems, it is to humble us and not to tumble us' OR 'If destiny hands you a lemon, choose to make lemonade.'

Fact Unfolded

Gopal Bhand was good-natured but a simpleton. His father was rather a learned peasant and always despaired for his plain son. "You must study hard, Gopal," he would tell his son, "Without learning, you will remain a frog in the well."

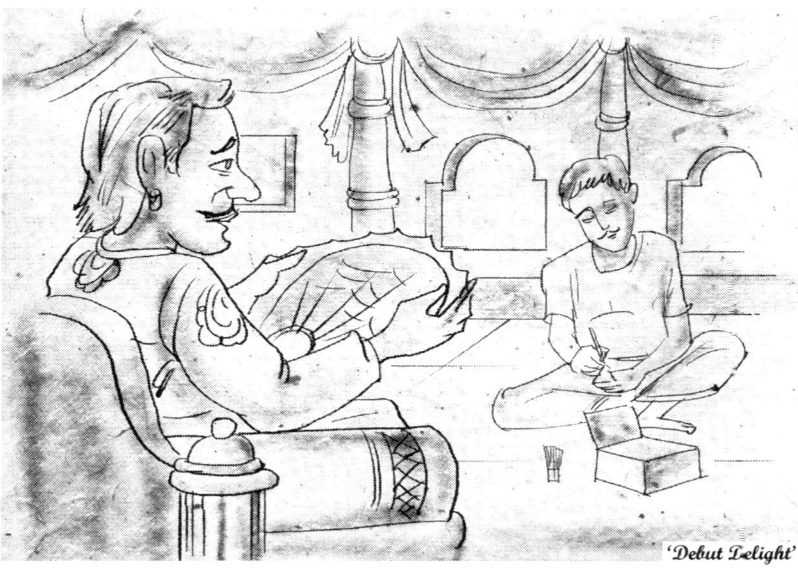

Poor Gopal tried very hard, but as destiny would have been, he could not progress much with his studies. Some years later, his father died. By then Gopal was married and had a family to look after. But no one would give him a job. Poor Gopal just carried the petty work of a village barber to earn his livelihood, but that also did not help him make his both ends meet.

One day, there was no food in the house and Gopal's wife fed up with their poverty said to him, "I have heard that Raja Krishna Chandra Rai of Nadia is very fond of good literature and felicitates scholars. Why don't you write a nice poem in his praise? Perhaps he will like it and give you a reward."

Gopal had no choice but to agree, and he immediately set off to have a bath in the pond before sitting down to write his verse. At the pond he saw a pig, covered in mud, rubbing its back against a tree trunk. The pig was rubbing its back so hard that Gopal was afraid its skin would come off. So the innocent Gopal said softly to himself, "You poor fellow... Don't rub so hard. It is not good for you. It will put your life in danger." Then, unable to think of anything else to write, he put down these words on a palm leaf and made his way to the *Rajbari*.

By the time he reached there, it was evening and the Palace gates were shut. The guard refused to let Gopal in. "Please," Gopal pleaded, "I have come from far off. I have an important document for the King." One of the guards took pity on him and agreed to leave the palm leaf where the King would see it in the morning.

Gopal handed over the palm leaf and went to rest in a dormitory. The royal guard placed the palm leaf on the King's table for him to see when he woke up.

The next morning, the royal barber came to trim the King's hair.

The barber sharpened his razor against a stone, while the King waited for his haircut. Just then, the King's eyes fell on the palm leaf and he read aloud what was written on it, "You poor fellow. . . . Don't rub so hard. It is not good for you. It will put your life in danger."

The barber had been sharpening his razor because he had already planned to use it to kill the King mysteriously. An evil courtier had made him agree to take on this wretched job of killing the King. When he heard the King's words, he was scared out of his wits. He thought that the King has come to know of his evil plan! He at once fell at the King's feet and begged for forgiveness. He also told the King about the courtier and how he had made the barber agree to carry out the King's killing.

The King got the cunning courtier arrested and threw him into prison. Then he realised that the words on the palm leaf had saved his life and he wanted to know who had written them. An astonished Gopal was dragged out of bed and presented before the King, who showered him with rewards and appointed him as the court astrologer.

A few days later in the Palace, the queen could not find her favourite necklace. The whole Palace was in turmoil. Even the King was worried. So he summoned Gopal. "Gopal, we know that you have marvellous powers to predict. You are an excellent astrologer. You saved my life with your divine powers. Now help us find the queen's necklace," he commanded.

Poor Gopal, he did not know what to do. Trembling he said, "I can look at the past and predict the future only when I am alone. Please let me go to my room. I will come to you shortly with the whereabouts of the necklace." Saying this, he rushed to his room, bolted the door and lamented to himself loudly, cursing his wife for the situation, "O lady, your desires have doomed your husband. Because of you, your husband is in trouble, and you may be a widow soon. Your husband escaped once, but this time there is no escape for him. The King is desperate for the lost necklace."

On the other side of the door, a maid-servant heard these words and started trembling. She had stolen an earring once with the help of her husband, who was the Palace gardener, and this time, the two had got greedy and stolen the queen's precious necklace. Hearing Gopal's words, she thought he was talking to her and knocked on his door. As soon as Gopal opened it, she fell at his feet and begged forgiveness. Then she told him where the necklace was and the earring were kept. Gopal happily went and told to the King about the whereabouts of the necklace and once again everyone marvelled at Gopal's divine powers.

A few weeks went by peacefully. Then one day, a messenger arrived from the neighbouring Kingdom. In his hand he held a wooden box, its lid shut tight. The messenger said, "We have heard much about the new astrologer in your *Rajbari* and his divine powers to predict. Here is a test. Can he tell what is in this box?"

The Court now turned towards Gopal. The Kingdom's reputation was hanging on his words. Gopal, who of course had no idea of what was in the box, muttered his father's words to himself, "Oh silly frog, your life is indeed becoming very difficult day by day."

No one understood what he meant, but the messenger looked amazed. He opened the lid and out hopped a frog!

By now the King was very impressed with Gopal and showered him with gold coins. But Gopal had enough. "I was told that I would be able to predict only three things correctly," he told the King, "I have finished making all three prophecies. Now please let me return to my wife."

The King didn't agree to send Gopal home. He not only plied him with many more gifts, but also bestowed upon Gopal the title of becoming the royal jester and a courtier to assist the King in his daily affairs.

This was how Gopal the barber gained entry into the *Rajbari* with his wit and intelligence and became the King's most adorned courtier.

Popular Version

We should major on minor things. Treat all difficulties as divine surgery and consider difficulties as a gift to look into what is happening more deeply. Pain then becomes a training ground for one to be more powerful. One has to become aware of the idea that most of our experiences of pain are just interpretations.

Learn to teach one-self as how to interpret in a powerful way and not a powerless way. If one interprets difficulties as pain, then one experiences them as pain and if one interprets difficulties as opportunities to grow, one will experience a great power within.

The Perfect Answer

Fact of the Matter

Life is a sequence of natural happenings. However, when we begin manipulating life according to our needs and requirements, then it doesn't remain a natural sequence. Something that is doctored becomes unnatural, stale and lifeless. The ability to see life and its beauty as 'it is' and not how 'it should be' is a great tool in living.

Fact Unfolded

Raja Krishna Chandra Rai was an Emperor of masses. Because of his proactive steps, the King was fondly renowned in whole Nadia. As another step towards providing better facilities to the public, the King

'A Political Superstar'

arranged to construct a huge water reservoir. After the completion of construction, he along with his few courtiers went to inspect the new reservoir. He asked his courtiers, "How does the water in this reservoir look like?"

To this Krishnananda Bachaspati, one of the courtiers said, "The water in this reservoir is so pure and natural."

Jagannath Tarkapanchanan, the second courtier remarked, "The water is crystal clear and is glittering."

Another courtier Hariram Tarkasiddhanta mentioned, "The water in the reservoir is marvellous. It is so splendid and gleaming."

Likewise, each of the other courtiers present there commented according to their own imaginations.

When Gopal Bhand's turn came, he stated to the King, "My Lord, the water has taken the shape of the reservoir you have built."

Without indulging in any exaggeration, Gopal Bhand just gave a relevant and pertinent answer. Raja Krishna Chandra liked his simple but basic talk and adorned him.

Popular Version

The craze to be 'extraordinary' is 'ordinary'. But to be 'ordinary' is in fact 'extraordinary'. There is greed to be unique, greed to be better than the other and hence, in this pursuit, one becomes bitter. To be simple is to drop the struggle of being better than the other. Dropping this complex desire to be unique makes life flowing and glowing. The wise one knows how to be simple and clean.

The Blame Game

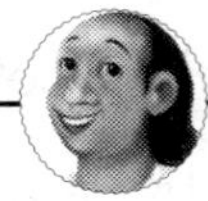

Fact of the matter

Blame game is rather foolishness. Instead one should endeavour to find resolution to the problem.

Fact Unfolded

One day, the customary *Rajbari*[1] was in progress. Raja Krishna Chandra and the courtiers were present there.

A shepherd came to the Court with a prayer. He said dejectedly,

'Shades of Reality'

---

1. *The Royal Court/Palace.*

"Your Highness, I request your help. I have come to your Court to seek justice."

"What has happened with you?" asked the King keenly.

"Your Majesty, yesterday one of the walls of my neighbour's house collapsed. As a result, my sheep got crushed under the collapsed wall and died straight away. I seek your kind help to get sufficient compensation from my neighbour because it is only my neighbour's fault which has done this unforeseen loss to me."

On hearing his appeal, Gopal Bhand got up and said, "Your Majesty, I don't think the neighbour can be blamed for the wall collapse."

"Then who is the real culprit in your opinion?" asked the King.

"Your Majesty, to find the real offender, we need to call the shepherd's neighbour to the *Rajbari* to inquire him," Gopal replied confidently.

The King agreed to Gopal's suggestion.

So the next day, the shepherd's neighbour was called in the *Rajbari* and asked to compensate the shepherd for the crushed sheep. The neighbour was a stingy farmer who replied in a soft tone, "You cannot blame me for this. The mason who built the wall should be blamed. He might have used weak material because of which the wall collapsed."

Listening to this, the mason was called to the *Rajbari*. Again he was asked to compensate for the crushed sheep. At this the mason said irritably, "How can you blame me? It was the labourer who mixed a thin watery batter of cement which perhaps could not hold up the bricks in the wall and the wall collapsed. You must ask him to pay for it."

So the labourer was summoned to the *Rajbari*. When he was asked to compensate for the loss of the shepherd, the labourer declared, "I am not to be blamed for this. It was the water-man who poured the extra water in the mortar. He must be caught and made to compensate."

Thus, the waterman was called and was asked to compensate. He said, "Sire, it's not my fault. The water-carrier which I use is very big in size. It holds more water than the amount required."

"Who gave you the water-carrier?" asked Gopal Bhand. "Sire, this shepherd had given me the water-carrier," said the waterman at once.

Gopal then looked at the shepherd and said, "Look, nobody else should be blamed. It's only your fault. Your one wrong step led to the collapse of the wall and thus the loss of your sheep."

The shepherd felt embarrassed and left the *Rajbari*. The King and his courtiers had a smile on their faces to see Gopal's wit and sense of justice.

Popular Version

If something goes wrong, it is more important to talk about who is going to mend it rather than who is to blame.

Mind Muscle

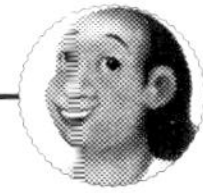

Fact of the Matter

Always be a possibility thinker.

Fact Unfolded

One summer afternoon, Taraknath, a merchant from Murshidabad was on his way to Krishnanagar with his mare carrying two sacks of wheat. After a long journey under the sun, he felt tired. So he along with his mare rested under an old banyan tree. When he woke up from his nap, he could not see the mare and started searching for it everywhere. While searching his mare, he met Gopal whom he asked, "Mister! I could not find my mare. Have you seen my mare

'At loggerheads'

anywhere?" To this Gopal immediately asked Taraknath, "Is your mare's right foot lame? Is its left eye blind? Is it carrying a load of wheat?"

Hearing this, Taraknath was happy and instantly said, "Yes, exactly! Please tell me where have you seen my mare?" Gopal answered, "I haven't seen it anywhere."

This made Taraknath very angry who started arguing with Gopal. As the quarrel intensified, he took Gopal to the King for punishment.

The matter reached the King. At the Royal Court, the King listened to the incident and asked, "Dear Gopal, if you had not seen the mare, how could you describe it?" Gopal answered, "Sire, I simply saw the tracks of a mare and noticed that the right and left tracks were different. From this, I understood that the mare that had just passed from there was limping. And the grass on the right side of the path was eaten but the grass on the left was not. From that I simply understood that the mare would be blind in its left eye. Further, there were wheat seeds scattered all around the ground from which I understood that it must have been carrying a load of wheat."

The King understood Gopal's cleverness and told Taraknath to excuse him.

Popular Version

Imagination, inspiration and commitment to excel are the mother of creativity. Imagination ushers wellness. Albert Einstein rightly said, 'Imagination is more important than knowledge.' So experience the experience of imagination.

Blind Greed

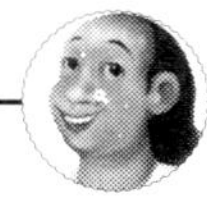

Fact of the matter

Business thrives on honesty and honesty arrives from morality.

Fact Unfolded

In Tehetta lived a rich landlord named Adhusudan. Due to an ailment, Adhusudan was going blind. To get himself cured, Adhusudan called for a renowned physician Balendranath from Kaliganj. Adhusudan told Balendranath that if he restored his failing eyesight, he would pay him heftily. However, if Balendranath couldn't cure the ailment, he would get nothing. The cunning physician noted that Adhusudan

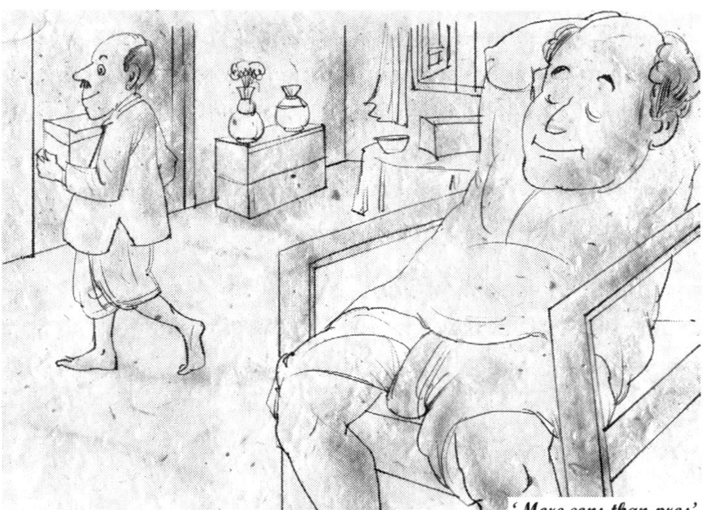

'More cons than pros'

had many expensive things in his grand house and greedily agreed to the deal.

From the next day, Balendranath started visiting Adhusudan with his *aushadi*[1] and started applying a *concoction*[2] to the eyes of Adhusudan every day as a part of medication. And noticing that Adhusudan could not see with the *concoction* over his eyes, Balendranath stealthily started taking away one object every day!

After a few days of his treatment and having taken with him the last precious object, Balendranath declared, "You are completely cured and can see everything! Now pay me what we agreed upon!"

Adhusudan saw that all the valuable objects were missing from his house. Realising what had happened, Adhusudan was perturbed. So he refused to pay anything to the physician. After heated arguments, both decided to take the matter to the *Rajbari*[3].

At the *Rajbari*, Raja Krishna Chandra Rai listened to both and sought the advice of Gopal Bhand for a just decision. Gopal noticing the deceitful intentions of Balendranath declared, "Adhusudan promised to pay Balendranath only if he restored Adhusudan's sight. Before Adhusudan became blind, he could see various objects present in his house. Now, with his sight restored, he sees them no longer. This means that he is still blind! Why then should he pay Balendranath?"

Listening to Gopal, Balendranath felt ashamed of his evil intentions but the Court cheered at the well-judged decision of Gopal and lauded him.

---

1. *Ayurvedic medicines*
2. *A thick paste of medicines*
3. *The Royal Court/Palace*

Popular Version

No business can prosper on immoral grounds. Immorality is the first sign of downfall of any system. The head of any organisation has to imbibe morality as the first and foremost trait. This becomes significant in the present context when the country is witnessing scams after scams being unearthed one after the other making the nation cripple with rampant corruption in all walks of life. Therefore, we should be morally strong.

Smarter Way

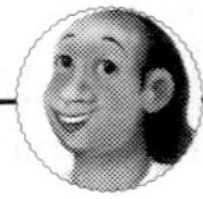

Fact of the Matter

A word is only a pointer pointing out the pointed. We should know how to go out wisely and take in wisely.

Fact Unfolded

Eknath, a close friend of Gopal Bhand, enjoyed hunting. Once he visited Krishnanagar and brought Gopal a hunted hare as a present.

Gopal took the hare to his wife, had her roast it in the way he most relished, and invited Eknath to stay and share it with him.

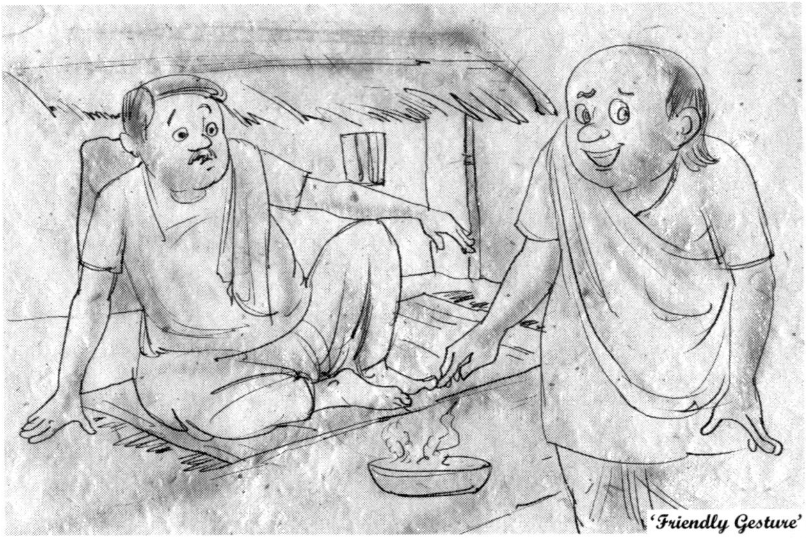

'Friendly Gesture'

Some days later, a man knocked at Gopal's gate. "Who is it?" called Gopal. "I am Lakshman Sen from Gayespur and a neighbour of your good hunter friend Eknath, who brought you the hare the other day," the man exclaimed. Gopal asked him in and let him rest and most hospitably set a great meal before him.

Not long after this, another stranger in country clothes called on Gopal at his house. "Who are you?" asked Gopal. "I am Ballal Dutt from Nabadwip and a close friend of Lakshman Sen, the neighbour of hunter Eknath who gave you the hare," said the stranger.

"Welcome, welcome," said Gopal and led him inside. When the guest was comfortably seated, Gopal placed in front of him a steaming bowl of hot water. "What is this?" asked the stranger. "Oh neighbour of the neighbour of the man who had given me the hare," he said, "this is the delicious soup of the soup of the hare that my good hunter friend, whose neighbour you know, brought me the other day. You can have it," said Gopal smilingly.

Ballal Dutt understood Gopal's satire and quickly left the place without uttering a word.

Popular Version

More than the length of words, it is the depth that touches others. Or else words don't have the desired impact. Proper use of words is objectifying which falls back more and more upon the subjective.

Chasing A Dream

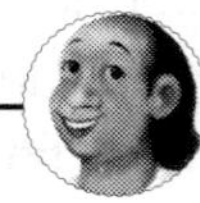

Fact of the matter

For optimum results efforts are consistently required.

Fact Unfolded

In Krishnanagar, Gopal Bhand lived just next door to a poor couple who had a peculiar habit of day-dreaming.

One day, the husband said to his wife: "If I had some money, I would certainly buy a few cows."

'Misfortune lives next door to stupidity'

"Then of course we would have a lot of milk," said his wife excitedly. "I could then make lots of *Mishti Doi*[1] and *Payesh*[2] all through the year and shall also have plenty of butter and ghee. We could then also send some milk to my sister in Santipur."

"Send milk to your sister!" exclaimed the husband. "How dare you suggest such a thing?"

"But we would have milk to spare," said the wife timidly.

"We'll sell it for a profit!" said the husband. "I don't want any more talk on this subject. Make sure you don't carry any milk to her when I'm away! If your dare to send her any milk, I'm going to break every pot in the house!" And picking up the four or five pots they had, he irritably smashed them on the floor, breaking them into pieces.

Gopal Bhand, who was just passing by, asked the reason for breaking the pots. When Gopal learnt the reason behind smashing the pots, he picked up a stick lying nearby and started beating the air with it.

Seeing Gopal behaving in an unusual manner, the puzzled neighbour asked surprisingly, "What are you doing?!"

"I am just driving away your cows!" said Gopal. "They've eaten all the cucumbers growing in my garden."

"Eaten your cucumbers!" exclaimed the neighbour in annoyance. "But you don't even have a garden! Then what to talk of cucumbers?"

"I'm going to have one soon," said Gopal, "and I'm going to grow cucumbers in it," and he continued hitting out with the stick again.

---

1. Sweet yoghurt
2. Rice pudding

The neighbours finally realised that Gopal was trying to show them how foolish it was to live in a world of make-believe and felt ashamed of themselves.

Popular Version

Hard work, endurance and perseverance – these traits are the simple ingredients to accomplish success. None can substitute these. This receipe is universal doctrine and has been honestly followed by all successful people whether explorers, yogis, karm yogis, illumined individuals or organisations. Our great leaders from Abraham Lincoln to Mahatma Gandhi all firmly believed that fortune sides with the person who dares.

Dangerous Liaison

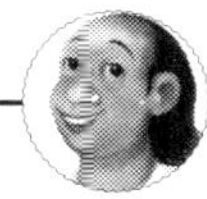

Fact of the Matter

To know and not to act on what you know is equal to not knowing.

Fact Unfolded

One fine day, when the King was busy playing chess with his wife, Rani Bhabani, Gopal Bhand came near them, saluted them, sat down, and watched the game. Slowly he took a fat *Hilsha*[1] from his bag which he had brought especially for the King.

'Message for masses'

1. *Fish is an admired cuisine among Bengalis. Hilsha is an oily and tropical fish which is most popular among Bengalis.*

The King got very impressed to see the luscious fish and ordered to give Gopal 1,000 gold coins as reward. For such reward, the King's wife criticised him, "This is a big amount for Gopal because every day you have to give rewards to scholars in the Palace and cities; and when you will give them less than this reward amount they will feel humiliated and may say that are they not even equal to Gopal the barber; and if you give them more, the Royal Treasury will be empty in a few days."

The King liked his queen's suggestion, so he asked, "Now what do I do?"

"Call Gopal and put a strange riddle to him. Ask him if the fish is a male or female. If he says it is female, say you don't like it; if he says it is male, again say you don't like it. Helpless, he will go; take his fish and reward away."

Pandit Baneswar Bidyalankar, a witty courtier in the *Rajbari*[2] just sitting close by and listening to the queen's suggestions, whispered to the King, "Don't be deceived by a woman. Don't depress Gopal. He is very loyal to Your Majesty."

But the King didn't listen to Bidyalankar. He called Gopal and asked, "Is the fish male or female?" Gopal said, "This fish is neither male nor female, actually, it is a eunuch."

The King was happy with his answer. He ordered to give 1,000 gold coins more as reward to Gopal. Gopal took the coins and put them in his purse. But when he was descending the palace stairs, one of the gold coins fell out on the floor.

Gopal just bent and picked it up. Seeing this, the Queen said, "How low-natured is this person that he can't even part with one coin."

2. *The Royal Court/Palace*

The King thought this behaviour of Gopal to be bad, so he called him. Again Pandit Baneswar Bidyalankar warned the King, "Don't stop him. Let him go."

But the King didn't agree. He called Gopal and said rudely, "How low and base is your heart that you are not even ready to let the *Rajbari's* attendants have one coin from such a hefty reward amount."

Gopal saluted again and said, "I am not base, but I know how to value grace. That is why I picked up the gold coin which felt accidentally. On one side of the coin is a holy verse from the Hindu scriptures and on the other side is engraved the King's honourable and illustrious name. If it is left on the ground, then it is certain that it will come under the foot of someone, and this is sheer disrespect which is not tolerable to me."

The King again became very happy to listen to Gopal's reply and ordered to give Gopal another 1,000 gold coins as reward.

Pandit Baneswar said, "Didn't I say don't stop him?"

The King smilingly said, "I am crazier than you because you stopped me twice, but I did not listen to you. By following this woman, I suffered this loss."

Popular Version

Parables, tales and narratives from time immemorial illustrate the universal truth – 'Learned fools are kings among fools'. Raja Krishna Chandra though knowing Gopal's cleverness miserably suffered the loss effortlessly due to his state of thoughtlessness and emptiness.

In the Red

Fact of the Matter

Don't poke your nose here and there. Keep confined to your own acts and deeds.

Fact Unfolded

Gopal Bhand had a very rich but miserly neighbour. This neighbour and his servants had a very bad habit of peeping into Gopal's house secretly. Once Gopal, while praying at his home, was saying, "Oh my Lord, give me one thousand gold coins. I beg for only one thousand coins and not even one less than a thousand! If it's missing one, I won't accept it."

'Inviting Trouble'

As usual, the tightfisted neighbour along with his attendants peeped into Gopal's house and heard Gopal asking God for the money. The neighbour said to his attendants, "Maybe I will experiment to see if Gopal is honest or not in what he says. I will toss to him only five hundred gold coins." And he took a bag of five hundred coins and threw it into the house of Gopal.

Gopal who was praying saw the bag of coins, and he said, "God! Thank you. . . . You gave me what I requested. You gave me a thousand gold coins! And that too so soon!" But when he began to count it, he found it only five hundred gold coins. So he said, "Oh my Lord, I asked you for one thousand and you gave me only five hundred, but I will accept these five hundred coins now. I accept it because you will surely give me another five hundred later."

But Gopal's neighbour became angry because Gopal took the five hundred gold coins! He thought, 'Maybe he won't take the money.' So he came and knocked on Gopal's house, "Hey Gopal, peace be upon you."

Gopal said, "Peace be upon you too. What do you want, Sire?"

The neighbour said, "I want those five hundred gold coins which you have received a while ago, for they are mine!"

Gopal said, "It was God who gave it to me and not you?" The neighbour said, "It was only me who threw the money to you."

Gopal said, "No, no Sire. It was only God who threw the money to me. I asked God and He gave it to me. I asked Him for one thousand gold coins, and He gave me five hundred coins today, and next week He'll surely give me the remaining five hundred."

And the neighbour said to him, "No, no. It's my money. You can ask my servants also for this." Gopal replied, "No, no, no, no."

The neighbour threatened, "I will go to the King for settling the matter."

When Gopal remained adamant to his belief, the rich neighbour said to Gopal, "Come on, we're going to the King."

Gopal said, "No, no. I can't; I'm tired. I can't walk. No ..... I don't even have a horse; I don't have anything at all to ride."

The neighbour said, "I will give you a horse. You ride it and we'll go to the King."

Gopal took the horse and said, "But.. no, no! I can't go because it's cold and I don't have any clothing. I am just having this *gamchha*[1] to protect myself from the cold wind."

The neighbour said, "I will give you a great outfit – a silken *sherwani*[2]. That will surely protect you from the cold weather"

Gopal said, "Ok, maybe," and he took the *sherwani* and just walked forward to ride the horse. Then he said, "No, no. I'm not going. I can't go with these shoes! These shoes are no good in front of the King! No, no. I can't. You must give me new shoes."

The neighbour replied, "Ok, that's possible. Here, I give you new shoes." Gopal took the horse, the *sherwani* and new shoes, and they went straight to the King. They arrived at the *Rajbari*[3] and said to the King, "Peace be upon you, Oh Raja,"

---

1. *A Gamchha is the local term for a sweat towel. It is a thin, coarse, traditional cotton towel quite popular in India especially in Bengal. It is used to dry the body after bathing or wiping sweat. Gamchha is often worn on one side of the shoulder.*
2. *Sherwani is a long coat-like garment worn in South Asia. It is traditionally associated with the Muslim aristocracy of the North Indian subcontinent.*
3. *The Royal Court/Palace*

The King asked the neighbour, "What do you want?"

The rich neighbour said, "Your honour, I gave Gopal five hundred gold coins. But he doesn't want to give me back those five hundred coins. That's my money!"

The King asked, "Is this true, Gopal?" Gopal said, "No, no, no. No, he's a liar."

The neighbor said, "No, I'm not a liar!"

Gopal said, "Hey King, look, maybe he'll tell you that this horse is his horse."

And the rich man immediately said, "Yes! It's my horse!"

Gopai said to the King, "Look! He's crazy! Maybe he'll say that this *sherwani* also belongs to him!"

And the rich man said, "Yes! It is my *sherwani*! I gave it to you!"

Gopal said, "He's crazy! Maybe he now says that these shoes are also his."

The neighbour said, "True! And these are also my shoes, not his shoes!"

Gopal said, "Look, oh King, at this madman!" The King got angry and said, "Get out! You're a liar!"

The neighbour went home with a sullen face. Later Gopal met the neighbour and said, "Come and take your money, your horse, your *sherwani* and your shoes; but I want you to know that I'm the winner. You are just stingy and rich and, therefore, take back everything. And next time, please, if I talk to God, don't intervene between me and Him. Only I am between me and God. I don't want some stingy neighbour interfere between me and God."

The neighbour listened to Gopal and quietly left the place with his belongings to be never seen interfering thereafter.

Popular Version

Unnecessary interference in others' acts only invites problems to oneself. To mind your own business is praiseworthiness.

Just
Like That

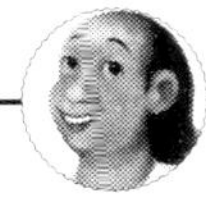

Fact of the Matter

What changes do you need to make in your thinking, emotional reactions, and actions?

Fact Unfolded

Gopal Bhand had a friend named Satinath. Though silly, Satinath always pretended to be smart.

One day, Gopal said to Satinath, "Could you please go to the store in the market for me and buy a canister (can) of milk. And if they have fish, get six."

'Talking Straight'

A while later, Satinath returned with six milk canisters. Gopal astonishingly asked, "Why the hell did you buy six canisters of milk?"

"They had fish Gopal," Satinath said. Gopal did nothing but smiled at his stupidity.

The very next day, Satinath brought a nice wooden chair for his house. To get rid of his old chair, he put it in his front yard and hung a signage on it saying: *'Free to good home. You want it, you take it. . . .'*

For three days, the chair sat there without anyone looking at it twice. Getting fed up, he went straight to Gopal for advice.

Gopal understood that people were too mistrustful of this deal. So to help his stupid friend, Gopal made Satinath change the signage to read: *'Chair for Sale – Only for 5 Gold Coins.'*

Satinath did as advised. The next morning someone stole it!

Popular Version

Most people react; they do not respond. Response is action. Action is a conscious decision; reaction is an act of impulsiveness.

Load-Sharing

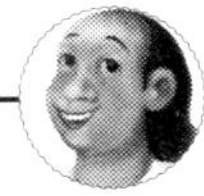

Fact of the Matter

The business of the prudent self is to get rid of the wickedness and not supervise it.

Fact Unfolded

Gopal Bhand often used his wit to teach people a lesson. Once he met Bijoy, the milkman. Bijoy cheated his customers by adding water in the milk and selling it to the innocent customers.

'A Fine Sight'

One day, Bijoy was carrying a large mud pot on his head, filled with milk. As soon as he saw Gopal he said, "You think you are so clever! But you won't be able to cheat me."

Gopal smiled and said, "Bijoy, why should I cheat you? Particularly today, the sky is very cloudy! It will rain any moment and I don't want to get drenched in the rain."

"Oh, I have a long way to go! My customers might be eagerly waiting for me. Is it going to rain?" Bijoy said hurriedly, and forgetting the pot on his head, looked up. The pitcher fell and broke, and the milk spilt all over the road.

That day Bijoy could not sell his milk-mixed-with-water to anyone!

Popular Version

Supervising immorality does not make it good. Always teach your inner apparatus to not allow any malice to be practiced. Attempt this world to make a fine place to live.

Loop in A Loop

Fact of the Matter

Bitter truths which amount to cheating or falsification of facts and create disharmony must be avoided.

Fact Unfolded

One winter afternoon, Kaliranjan, the crafty landlord, went to the market for buying firewood. There he found an old, naïve villager named Deveedaas. "Five coins for the cart," said Deveedaas to Kaliranjan, thinking he was making a good bargain.

'Plans go awry'

“Sure, sure,” said the cunning Kaliranjan, “so be good to deliver it to my house.”

When Deveedaas had deposited the firewood in Kaliranjan’s courtyard, he got into the cart to drive his bullocks home.

“Not so fast,” said Kaliranjan, “why are you taking away my property?”

Deveedaas looked at Kaliranjan in amazement. But Kaliranjan started shouting, “Don’t look so surprised, you old rascal. You said five coins for the cart, so I get the firewood, the cart and the bullocks that were drawing it.”

“But you know what it meant,” said Deveedaas, who was nearly in tears, “Nobody sells firewood, a cart and a pair of bullocks for five coins. I will be ruined.”

“Nonsense,” said Kaliranjan, “you gave your word and you must keep it, otherwise God himself will punish you.”

Deveedaas fell at Kaliranjan’s feet, but Kaliranjan would not relent. So the old villager walked the long way home feeling sad and desperate. When his sons heard the story, they were furious. They grabbed some sticks and said they were going to thrash the landlord.

But the oldest son said, “No, let’s go to the wise Gopal Bhand and get an advice to do it in another way.”

So they went to Gopal and told him their sad story. Gopal agreed to teach the landlord a lesson.

Gopal told Deveedaas, “I will need another cart of firewood to take to the market tomorrow.”

Deveedaas agreed and gave Gopal a cart full of firewood.

Next day, Gopal disguised himself as a poor villager, went to the marketplace and found Kaliranjan there. When he saw the poor villager bringing firewood into the market in his cart, Kaliranjan said to himself, 'Ah ha, another village idiot especially for me,' and rubbed his hands together in delight just as cunning landlords do, and went up to poor villager.

"Two handfuls of coins for the firewood," said the poor villager. Kaliranjan was very pleased. He was going to get an even better bargain today. While telling the villager to deliver the wood at his house, Kaliranjan promised himself that he would put only one very small coin in each of his hands.

Kaliranjan emerged from his home with his fists closed. "Take your money," he said to Gopal who had delivered the wood at his courtyard. But to his astonishment, Gopal held on to Kaliranjan's fists and would not let go. "What are you doing?" Kaliranjan yelled.

"Why are you shouting?" said Gopal calmly, "You promised me a fistful of coins. So I get the pennies and the fists." Saying this, Gopal picked up an axe from a nearby idol of a deity decorated in Kaliranjan's courtyard and said, "Stand still. I am going to cut off your hands."

Kaliranjan screamed and begged, but Gopal said, "Yesterday that old man begged you to return his cart and bullocks but you refused. If I cut off your hands, yesterday's debt and today's both will be met."

Kaliranjan begged forgiveness and offered to give Gopal ten gold coins, and also return Deveedaas' cart and bullocks. Gopal laughed. "Want any firewood tomorrow?" he asked Kaliranjan cheekily. And he took away the two carts to give them to Deveedaas.

Popular Version

The balance sheet of every life is tallied and updated every second. This is the law of nature. So don't grow fast, grow well. Deep root, sweet fruits.

The Penicillin inventor Alexander Fleming's father reportedly saved Winston Churchill from drowning. Out of gratitude, Churchill's father paid for young Fleming's education. Later, his invention helped save the young Churchill's life. So 'goodness begets goodness' and 'evil begets evil'.

Lucrative Business

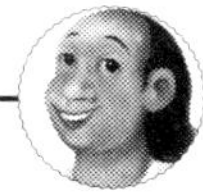

Fact of the Matter

Kind actions begin only with kind feelings.

Fact Unfolded

One day an Arabian businessman met Gopal Bhand in Krishnanagar and said, "Dear *Sheikh*[1] Gopal! I want to set up a business in Krishnanagar. You are the cleverest person I know in this city. Please give me an advice as to what should I buy that would benefit me the most."

Gopal calmly replied, "Iron and cotton."

'Real and Unreal'

1. *Sheikh or Shaykh is an honorific term in the Arabic language that literally means 'wise' or 'elder' or noble'.*

The businessman went away and bought a consignment of iron and cotton and stocked them. After a few months, he sold them and gained plenty of profit. After a few days, again he met Gopal and said, "O Crazy Gopal! What should I buy that would profit me?"

This time Gopal told him to buy onions and watermelons. The businessman went and bought his entire savings worth of onions and watermelons. Just a few days later, they all rotted and caused a lot of loss to the businessman.

He immediately sought out Gopal and said, "When I first asked you for an advice, you told me to buy iron and cotton. I profited a lot from this, but the second time what kind of advice did you give me! All my wealth is destroyed!"

Gopal said, "The first day you addressed me as 'Sheikh Gopal', and since you addressed me as an intelligent person, I advised you according to my wisdom. The second time you called me 'Crazy Gopal', so I advised you like a crazy person."

The businessman was ashamed of his behaviour and understood Gopal thoroughly.

Popular Version

In this age of profiling, where everyone seeks to succeed by categorising, the greatest pillar of understanding is that compassion and love are contagious. Thoughts and feelings of affection can be spread as an infection. Because 'respect begets respect', we need to deepen awareness to the fact of giving respect to others. Learn to give thoughts and feelings of affection even to a stranger. Then you will find true happiness.

New Ideas

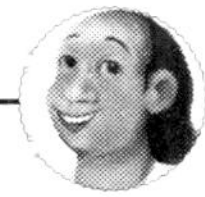

Fact of the Matter

Life in bits and pieces may be bitter but we can make it something fascinating with our creativity.

Fact Unfolded

Once after a good fishing on River *Jalangi*[1], Gopal Bhand was walking from the river banks carrying two succulent *hilsha*[2] in a bucket.

'Mutual Admiration'

1. *Jalangi River is a branch of Ganges in Bengal which flow into the Hooghly.*
2. *Fish is an admired cuisine among Bengalis and hilsha is an oily tropical fish and most popular among Bengalis.*

Seeing Gopal carrying the fish, a *Rajbari*[3] Sepoy approached him and enquired as to whether Gopal possessed the required permission for fishing along the public coastline?

At this Gopal replied, "Sire, let me clarify your doubts. I am not here to fish. I did not even catch these *hilsha*. Rather they are my pets. Every day I come down to the seashore and put these fish into the river waters and take them for a long walk to the end of the shore and back. When I'm ready to go, I whistle and they immediately jump back into the bucket and we go home together."

The Royal Sepoy, obviously, did not believe him and he reminded Gopal that it was absolutely illegal to fish along the public seashore without obtaining permission from the Authority. Gopal turned to the Sepoy and said calmly, "If you don't believe me, then watch," saying this, Gopal threw both the *hilsha* back into the river waters.

The Sepoy said, "Now whistle to your fish and show me that they will jump out of the water into your bucket."

Gopal turned to the Sepoy and said, "What fish?" and walked away quietly leaving the Royal Sepoy gaping.

Popular Version

Creativity or creative thinking is not merely an act but an approach. It is a sacred approach which makes us look things differently. It is a quality that we need to bring in our normal activities of life.

❁❁❁

3. *The Royal Court/Palace*

On a Slippery Track

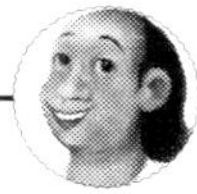

Fact of the Matter

Honesty and truthfulness are indeed the basic morals and foremost ethical values to be practiced in our lives.

Fact Unfolded

Once, Keerthinath, the *Zamindaar*[1] of Krishnanagar, went to buy some cattle at the *Poush Mela*[2] in nearby Birnagar. At the fair, he

'After Bumps, A Smooth Ride'

1. *Zamindaars were an aristocratic and typically hereditary class who lived during pre-Independent India and held enormous tracts of land.*
2. *Poush Mela is an important seasonal festival held during end-December in Bengal.*

found some very fine cattle which he ought to buy. But he found that he had forgotten to bring any money along with him. He did not want to wait till the next day, as the cattle could be sold to someone else. So he decided to ask Debjit, the local moneylender for help.

Debjit agreed to lend money to Keerthinath. But he insisted that Keerthinath should leave something with him as a guarantee that the money would be returned. Keerthinath only had an old sword with him, which he said was quite precious as it had been inherited from his great-grandfather. He carried it with him to protect himself from robbers. He offered it to Debjit as a guarantee.

Debjit agreed to take the sword as guarantee, and gave Keerthinath the money he wanted. Keerthinath left, saying he would return the money in a few days.

A few days passed, a week, a month, and then several months. There was no sign of Keerthinath or the money. Debjit sent one of his trusted men to Keerthinath's house, but he always came back empty-handed. At all times, Keerthinath's servants would tell that their master was out hunting, or he had gone to visit his relatives, or he was ill and could not be disturbed and so on.

Tired of all these excuses, and worried about his money, Debjit decided to think of a way of getting his money back. There was no use asking for it any more.

After much thought, Debjit went to Gopal Bhand the clever barber. Debjit told his problem to Gopal and asked for help. Gopal listened and suggested a solution to Debjit.

As planned, the next day, Gopal told everybody who came to him for a haircut or for a shave, "I'm really afraid of the anger of Keerthinath the *Zamindaar*. He had given his ancestral sword to

Debjit, the moneylender of Birnagar as a guarantee in exchange for some money lent to him. While giving the sword, he told Debjit to take great care of it till he reclaimed it. It had belonged to Keerthinath's great-grandfather. I don't know how it happened, but Debjit has lost it. It's probably the fault of one of his useless servants, but now Debjit is really afraid and do not know what to say to Keerthinath about the sword. If Keerthinath comes to know of the lost sword, he would not spare Debjit."

Gopal would gossip about it to everyone who came to him for a haircut or a shave.

A few days later, when Keerthinath came to Gopal for a shave, Gopal told him the same story as well. Keerthinath pretended to be angry, but he was really very pleased. Now he would not have to return the money he owed to Debjit.

Next day, taking the money he owed to Debjit, Keerthinath went to his (Debjit's) house, and demanded his sword. Debjit fell at Keertinath's feet and asked for forgiveness because he had lost the sword. Keerthinath shouted in great anger. A small crowd gathered to watch.

"I don't know anything. I just want my ancestral sword. Go inside and look again," shouted Keerthinath, "I will not leave without my sword."

Debjit went into his house again, and after a while returned with the sword saying, "Oh, I am sorry. I had misplaced your previous sword. It was lying under my bed. Probably, my nasty servant has placed it over there. Sire, you can have it now." Keerthinath was upset. He would now have to pay back the money, especially with the crowd watching what he would do. Amidst the crowd, stood Gopal smiling sarcastically.

Popular Version

We should practice truthfulness and honesty in our daily conduct. We must stay away from profiteering or hoarding; must use the correct weights and measures and have clean bookkeeping. There is no parallel to honesty and truthfulness on this planet.

One For Many

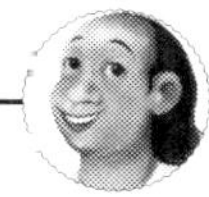

Fact of the Matter

Do not think of knocking out another person's brain because he differs in opinion from you.

Fact Unfolded

Four friends – Gurupada, Ramanath, Tanay and Sanjib lived in Kalyani town. All of them loved to make up bogus stories to befool and cheat innocent people.

Once during a winter evening, while returning to Krishnanagar

'Thick of Things'

after attending the Bera *Utsav*[1], Gopal decided to make a night halt at a highway Inn. When Gopal entered the Inn, he saw the four friends also staying there. Seeing Gopal dressed in fine clothes and carrying a bag full of articles, the four laid an evil eye and decided to play a trick to rob Gopal of his clothes and valuables.

Soon they went up to Gopal, offered him *Jhal Muri*[2] and started talking. "Where are you coming from, Sire?" they asked Gopal politely. The clever Gopal understood their bad intentions but anyhow behaved childlike.

Gopal smiled at the four friends affectionately and explained, "I have come from a distant land and I am returning home after making purchases from the *Bera Utsav.* Please tell me gentlemen, who you are?"

All the four introduced themselves to Gopal one by one in a friendly manner.

"I am from a village near Kutabpur," said Gurupada.

"My house is in the midst of a forest near Devagram which is full of wild animals," said Ramanath.

"I have my house near Bhagirathi River," said Tanay, "and you know that the mighty river is very long and difficult to cross."

"And I live on the top of the highest hill nearby Chakdaha," said Sanjib.

Gopal listened patiently to the four friends.

After a brief introduction, Gurupada suggested, "The night is too long and shivering. Why don't each one of us tell a story? In this

---

1. *Bera Utsav is a festival held at Lalbagh on the Bhagirathi River near the Palace of Nawabs every year during the Bengali month of Bhadra.*
2. *Jhal Muri is a tea time Bengali snack.*

way, we will not feel bored. The one whose story is not real will win. Others will have to do whatever the winner says."

Gopal agreed to the suggestion without any hesitation.

First Gurupada started, "Immediately after I was born, my mother asked my father to pluck some plums from the tree in front of the house. My father refused. I gently slipped out from my cot, climbed the tree, plucked the plums and placed a basketful at the kitchen door." He paused, and then continued, "My mother was very happy to see the plums, not knowing how they had come there. She ate as many plums as she liked and gave the rest to the neighbours." Narrating his story, Gurupada waited for a reply from Gopal, who only nodded his head slightly.

It was Sanjib's turn. "When I was a week old," he started, "I went for a walk in the forest. There I found a tree laden with ripe fruits. So I climbed up. I ate as many fruits as I wanted. I did not know how to climb down. So I went to the village searching for a ladder. I found a ladder which I put it against the tree and climbed down." After completing his story he also looked hopefully at Gopal who again just nodded his head.

A while after, Ramanath started his story: "I had my first adventure fairly late. When I was a year old, I chased a rabbit, but to my surprise, when the rabbit went into the jungle it turned into a tiger. So I told the tiger that if it wanted to eat me, it would not be fair because I had actually chased a rabbit and not a tiger. But it pounced on me. So I caught its jaw and tore it into two." Ramanath looked at Gopal who only nodded silently.

As each one of them told his story one after another making Gopal fully occupied in their tales, the four secretly managed to get hold of Gopal's bag of articles and clothes and hid it with themselves. Gopal observed this wicked act but pretended to have not seen anything and continued to listen to them with deep interest.

The story session continued further. "Last year," said Tanay, "I took a boat and went fishing. There were other fishermen also but none of us could catch a single fish. I left the boat and dived into the river. Down and down I went. After three or four hours, I touched the river bottom. Then to my horror I saw a huge fish, swallowing all other fishes. Before it could see me, I charged and gave it a mighty blow with my fist. The fish was dead. As I was hungry, I made a fire, roasted the fish, and ate it all by myself. Then I floated back and told the other fishermen of my adventure."

Again Gopal simply nodded.

Now it was Gopal's turn. He cleared his throat, popped a few *Jhul Muri* snacks in his mouth and began his story.

"Some years ago I had a cotton farm in which there was a big tree, bright red in colour. For a long time, the tree was barren with no branches or leaves, but after sometime it grew four branches. On each branch there grew a bud which turned into a big fruit. I plucked the fruits, but when I cut them open, to my surprise, I saw that a young man jumped out from each fruit. The four young men grew in my farm and became my slaves."

His listeners nodded in surprise. Gopal continued, "I put them to work on the farm. I soon found that they were very lazy and would not work until I gave them a good beating."

Gopal paused for a moment to watch their faces. Then he continued. "One day I had to go to Hanskhali town to purchase seeds. On my return I found that they all had run away. Since then

I have been looking for them. How lucky I am that I have found you four at last! Young men, you have to come back to my farm. You know that you are my slaves."

The four young men looked at each other in surprise. They knew that they had lost the bet. If they said that they believed him, then they had to become Gopal's slaves; and if they disbelieved, as per the condition laid by them in the beginning of the story session, they had to do as Gopal wished. All four were confused. They therefore said that Gopal could have his wish.

Gopal said smilingly, "I do not want anything from you. Neither I want to have you at my farm. I just want to make you learn a lesson. Just give me my clothes and valuables. Not only that, give me your clothes also." The four young men quickly agreed and returned Gopal's stolen bag. They also removed their clothes and gave them to Gopal.

Gopal made a big bundle of their clothes and walked away making the cloth-less young men shiver all night repenting for their misdeeds with each passing moment.

Popular Version

Don't just be a victim of an experience but be a victor. Life is not a problem, but a mystery. Watch carefully – Many things in life are beyond our comprehension. Deceit, greed and treachery should be dealt with an iron hand. He that cheats shall be cheated.

One-on-One

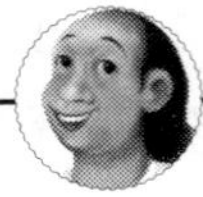

Fact of the Matter

Don't keep a Tally Sheet. Free thinking sustains laughter. We owe much to free thinking.

Fact Unfolded

Once, Gopal Bhand accompanied the royal entourage during the King's routine trip to the countryside. The King observed the countryside with curiosity, so did Gopal. On seeing the fields, Gopal pointed to some cows and said to the King, "It's going to rain." The King looked at him and asked eagerly,"How can you say that Gopal?"

'Leaving no loose end'

"They say that if cows are lying down, it means rain, and if they are standing up, it will be dry," Gopal explained the King.

A little later, they saw more cows, some lying down and others standing. At this, the King sarcastically asked Gopal to make his forecast about the weather. Gopal paused for a moment to give his latest weather forecast. He then declared confidently, "Scattered showers!" The King was startled to hear Gopal's weather forecast.

After moving a mile further, the entourage came across a crowd gathered around the village pond and making a hue and cry. The King immediately instructed the accompanying courtier Krishnananda Bachaspati to inquire into the matter.

Bachaspati went close to the crowd and inquired. He returned and explained, "Sire, one of the village landlords has accidentally fallen into the pond and is crying hoarse for help. The villagers have gathered to help him but the landlord is not ready to get out. Everybody is confused for his strange act."

The King was perplexed. Gopal who was also listening to the act said, "Let me give a try."

Gopal immediately dismounted his horse, went close to the pond where the landlord had fallen and said something to him. Soon, the landlord was seen holding Gopal's hand and coming straight out of the pond, drenched and breathless. The villagers cheered and made the landlord comfortable.

Gopal returned to the King and mounted the horse. The King surprisingly asked, "Gopal, did you know that strange fellow?" "No Sire!" replied Gopal. "He seems to be a strange fellow. He was reluctant to get out. Then how come you saved him within a minute?" inquired the King.

"Sire! That landlord is quite rich but a great miser. He is in a habit of just taking – be it things, money or favours. And he never gives anything to anyone. The innocent villagers in a bid to save him shouted and asked for his hand to pull him out the pond. But the miser landlord did not agreed to give his hand. I just offered him my hand for help. He immediately agreed to take my hand. In this way, I managed to save the miserly landlord by giving my hand and pulling him out of the pond," explained Gopal.

The King and the accompanying courtiers were amused to listen to Gopal's novel way of managing the problem by lending his hand for help.

Popular Version

There is a comic way of looking at the world and a comic way of expressing what you see. The comic vision is a way of looking at the incongruities and imperfections of the world. But this comic vision is the most difficult thing to have. It is almost inborn.

❋❋❋

Out of Sync

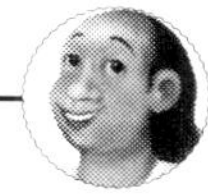

Fact of the Matter

We are unique and smart, so is our neighbour.

Fact Unfolded

Once, Gopal Bhand had a terrible day fishing on the lake, sitting in the blazing sun all day without catching even a single one. On his way home, he stopped at the *fishmonger*[1] and ordered him four *rohu*[2] fish.

'Making a Point'

1. A retailer of fish
2. A non-oily, fresh water and herbivore fish

He told the *fishmonger*, "Pick four large ones out and throw them at me, will you?"

"But why do you want me to throw them at you?" asked the *fishmonger* surprisingly.

"So that I am able to tell my wife, in all honesty, that I have caught the fish," said Gopal smilingly.

"Okay, but I suggest that you take the *hilsha*[3] instead of *rohu*," said the *fishmonger* aloud.

"Why's that?" asked Gopal amazingly.

"Simply because your wife came in earlier today and said that if you came by, I should tell you to take *hilsha*. That's what she would like for dinner tonight", replied the *fishmonger* with a grin.

Gopal did nothing but smiled to himself at the unique encounter he had.

Popular Version

It is not that your wit possesses broad spectrum immunity. There always exist antidotes for your wit and cleverness. And that too at only an arm's length.

---

3. *A popular oily and tropical fish.*

Play of The Day

Fact of the Matter

Jumping to conclusions is nothing but foolishness.

Fact Unfolded

Raja Krishna Chandra Rai always took advice of his wise jester – Gopal Bhand. Gopal was a clever and honest man who always gave good guidance, but he had one annoying habit. No matter what happened, he always said, "It is God's will. Everything God does is good."

Things came to a head when the King returned from war one day. He had been victorious, but during battle, he had lost a finger. When he came back to the *Rajbari*[1], feeling very sorry for himself, all courtiers wept and wailed, but Gopal said, "It is God's will. Everything God does is good."

'Lucky One'

1. *The Royal Court/Palace*

When the King heard these words of Gopal, he lost his temper. In a fit of rage, the King told Gopal to immediately leave the *Rajbari* and ordered that he should never return in front of him. Gopal was sad, but he had to do what the King had commanded.

One day, some months later, the King was out hunting again. He rode out far ahead of those who had accompanied him, and was caught by *thugs*[2]. The *thugs* were very happy to have such a special victim to make an offer to *Maa Kali*[3]. It wasn't everyday that a King came their way.

While, the *thugs* started to make preparations with fervor for the sacrifice, the King was in a grip of fear.

Suddenly, one of the *thugs*, who was guarding the King, cried, "Stop. ... We can't offer this fellow to *Maa Kali*. He isn't whole. We can only offer a human sacrifice to the Goddess which is complete and whole; otherwise *Maa Kali* will get annoyed."

Saying this, he showed the other *thugs* the stump on the King's hand where there should have been a finger. The *thugs* were very disappointed, but they decided to let the King go as he was of no use to them.

The King felt relieved. As the tired and thirsty King tried to find his way back to his Palace, he came upon a hut in the middle of the forest. He knocked on the door to ask for some water. When the door opened, he was amazed to find that it was Gopal, his admired court jester who lived there.

---

2. *Member of a well-organized grouping of professional and cruel assassins who travelled in gangs throughout India for several hundred years. Thugs were cheats and would imply themselves into the confidence of wayfarers and, when a favourable opportunity presented itself, strangle them by throwing a handkerchief or noose around their necks. They then plundered and buried them. Hindus thugs were worshipers of Maa Kali.*
3. *Maa Kali is the Hindu Goddess associated with eternal energy. Certain sects believe in the ritual that making human sacrifices (yagna) to Maa Kali is auspicious.*

"You were right, Gopal," the embarrassed King said humbly, "I was saved by the loss of that little finger. Yes, indeed, it is God's will. Everything God does is good." The King further added, "But Gopal, you haven't had much luck. God hasn't done so well to you. You were insulted by me and you suffered a lot."

"No Your Honour. It is God's will. Everything God does is good," said Gopal. "On the contrary, if I happened to be still with you, I would have to look for you in the forests when we thought you were lost. In that case, the cruel *thugs* would have caught me and sacrificed me in your place," Gopal explained smilingly.

The King laughed at Gopal exclamation and embraced Gopal. Then the King and Gopal went back to the *Rajbari*.

Popular Version

Do you just follow your ignorant mind? Words of wise should be chewed and then swallowed. Actions should emerge thereafter. Always remain open to the words of intelligent people. So don't grow fast, grow well. Deep roots, sweet fruits.

Precious View

Fact of the Matter

Solution always lies within the problem itself. What essentially required is inquisitive managerial sense to take stock of the situation to logically arrive at its solution.

Fact Unfolded

During the reign of Raja Krishna Chandra, there lived a splendid trader named Gobardhan who had three sons. A rich man, Gobardhan owned a herd of fine horses. Before he died, he told his sons, what

'Follow me who can'

they should do after his death, "When I die, my eldest son will take $\frac{1}{2}$ (one half) of the number of my horses; my second son will take $\frac{1}{4}$th (one forth) of the horses and my youngest son will take $\frac{1}{5}$th (one fifth) of the horses."

A few days later Gobardhan died. After the performance of the last rites, the three sons went back home to do what their father had told them. But when they had counted the horses, they noticed that the herd consisted of 19 odd horses. Of course, it was not possible for them to take $\frac{1}{2}$, $\frac{1}{4}$th or even $\frac{1}{5}$th of the total 19 horses as desired by Gobardhan.

At this, the three sons started to argue, but they couldn't find a solution. So they decided to visit the *Rajbari*[1]. At *Rajbari*, they explained their problem to Raja Krishna Chandra. Listening to the problem, the King also recognised that he wasn't able to solve their problem. In order to find a solution to the peculiar problem, he called Gopal Bhand to the *Rajbari*.

Gopal, a clever man was respected all over the Kingdom, especially for his fair and amicable decisions. After listening to the problem at the *Rajbari*, Gopal sent the three brothers back home and assured that he would visit their house the following day.

The next day, Gopal riding on his horse came to the brothers. The three brothers led Gopal to their stable. Gopal taking note of the horses standing in the stable said, "Well, you have got a total of 19 odd horses, don't you? Let's assume that my horse is also yours. Now, at this very moment you have a total of 20 horses. Isn't it? .... Now, we divide these horses as per your father's wish. So, $\frac{1}{2}$ of 20 is 10, so the eldest son would get 10 horses. Now, $\frac{1}{4}$th of 20 is 5, so the

---

1. The Royal Palace/Court

second son will get 5 horses. Lastly, $\frac{1}{5}$th of 20 is 4, so the youngest son will get 4 horses. Is that okay for you? This division is altogether as per your father's wish."

The three boys agreed contentedly. "Well," said Gopal, "10 plus 5 plus 4 equals 19 horses (10+5+4=19). So there is still a horse left. Look at that 20th horse, it's still mine." And saying this, Gopal gleefully climbed onto his horse and went away leaving everybody behind happy and satisfied.

Popular Version

You can let a bad situation overwhelm and embitter you, or you can decide what must be done, do it, and get on with your life. Learning, perception and problem solving — the dynamic interaction among these three is real and important for a preacher. As weather shapes mountains, problems too shape preachers. A preacher solves the problem by proper husbanding of available resources. After devising the solution, the preacher removes himself from the scene leaving the goal accomplished.

Call of Duty

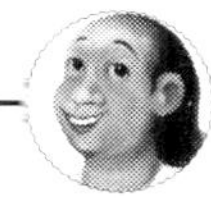

Fact of the Matter

Learn to develop the courage to be emotionally honest, or at least, don't defend your dishonesty.

Fact Unfolded

The loyal Gopal Bhand was made the *Khazanchi,* i.e. the Incharge of Royal Treasury by Raja Krishna Chandra Rai.

One day, with a candle burnt by his side, Gopal sat down meticulously recording all revenues and expenses of the Treasury.

Just then his close friends Debabrata and Bimal from Birnagar appeared. They always aspired to get some positions of authority in

'Nipping in the Bud'

the *Rajbari*[1] and had just come to strike a deal with Gopal. If Gopal recommended them to the King for the desired place of distinction in the *Rajbari*, they would in turn pledge their full support to Gopal in the affairs of the Treasury. Gopal knew well of this wickedness.

Just as they were to sit down, Gopal put out the candle burning beside him and lit another one.

Debabrata and Bimal exchanged a glance of surprise and then one of them said, "O Gopal, we have come here for some important business. But why did you extinguish the first candle to light another?"

Gopal replied thoughtfully, "That was a candle bought of Treasury funds. As long as I worked for the Treasury, I used it. Now you have come for some personal work, so I must use the candle bought of my personal funds."

Debabrata and Bimal felt ashamed. They realised what Gopal wanted to explain them. They quietly left the Treasury without uttering another word.

Popular Version

If you protect your dishonesty, then the truth only brings disturbance. Truth only reaches the honest. It is not the speed of your travel that matters on the road but the direction. Be happy even if you have to walk or jog so long as you are in the right direction. There is a saying in the *Yajur Veda: Sam jyotisha jyoti* or may light enhance light. And light can be enhanced only by honest conduct.

---

1. *The Royal Court/Palace*

The Ugly Truth

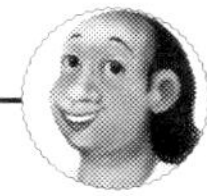

Fact of the Matter

To put it nicely though not precisely is tact. The secret of man's success exists in his insight into people's moods, and his tact in dealing with them.

Fact Unfolded

Once Benoy Bhushan, the renowned astrologer of *Nabadwip,* sat weeping profusely at the market corner. Noticing the sad state of Benoy, Gopal Bhand, who was just passing through the marketplace, enquired into the matter.

'There's Plenty to Cheer'

Benoy controlling his tears sadly explained, "The King specially called me to foretell his future. I closely studied his horoscope and told him that he had a great fortune and shall enjoy riches all through his life. But during his life time, he will see all his near and dear ones dying one after another due to one or the other reason. This will make the King sad. For foretelling this, the King instead of rewarding me, rebuked and insulted me and ordered to throw me out of city gates," Benoy wept. "Now tell me! Is telling truth a crime? My predictions can't be challenged and I have never spoken a lie or manipulated facts. Just for the reason that the King shall see his near and dear ones dying during his life time, he got irritated and bestowed insult upon me," Benoy continued to explain.

Gopal understood the entire incident. The next day he visited the *Rajbari*[1]. Gopal found the King to be upset and when asked, he told Gopal about Benoy's predictions. Gopal told the King that he knew one equally renowned *soothsayer*[2] from Chandannagar who predicts accurately. Apprising this, Gopal assured the King to make the soothsayer of Chandannagar visit *Rajbari* shortly.

After a week, Gopal disguised himself as a soothsayer named Balaichand from Chandannagar and visited *Rajbari*. Benoy Bhushan also disguised himself and accompanied Balaichand as his disciple.

In the *Rajbari*, after pretending to have perused the King's horoscope deeply, Balaichand explained, "Marvellous. . . ! I have never come across such a horoscope. Only riches, success, grandeur in Your Honour's life. All through life, Your Majesty will experience happiness and royalty. And much more ..the King'll live long. He will

---

1. The Royal Palace/Court
2. Fortune-teller

live longer and healthier than all his friends, relatives and near and dear ones."

This made the King cheerful and awarded a 1,000 gold coins to Balaichand.

Balaichand (Gopal) came out of *Rajbari* and handing over the reward to Benoy triumphantly said, "Have you seen? I have also told the truth to the King ...but tactfully. Always make a point without making an enemy. Make a person see the lightening without letting him feel the bolt. Understand." And saying this, Gopal bade him adieu.

Popular Version

Tact is one of the first mental virtues, the absence of which is often fatal to the best of talents. It is a kind of mental reading which often makes us deal with odd situations graciously. The sting of a bee is a convincing argument that 'spring' has arrived, but the brush of a butterfly's wing tells the same story in a more pleasant and tactful manner.

Thinking Out of The Box

Fact of the Matter

It is not wealth, nor ancestry, but thinking positive with a noble outlook that makes men great. A man endowed with a humane mind is the best kind of nobility.

Fact Unfolded

After attending the annual *Jhulan Mela*[1] in Nawabgunj, Gopal and his wife hired a cart for their journey back to Krishnanagar. During the

'Nothing to declare except genius'

1. *It is Bengal's oldest fair which falls during August-September. This fair draws thousands of people and ends on the day of Janmashthami.*

journey, they had to cross the mountainous terrain along the Jalangi River. While on the way, Gopal and his wife decided to get down the cart for paying obeisance at the nearby *Maa Laxmi* and *Maa Durga*[2] temples.

After Gopal and his wife got down, the cart moved on carrying other travellers. As the cart moved a short distance, a huge rock fell on the cart from the nearby mountain and crushed the cart to crumbs. Everybody on board was killed at once.

A large crowd gathered at the mournful incident. Gopal on seeing this tragedy said, "I wish we were on that cart."

Everyone in the crowd was surprised to hear Gopal's words. The crowd stunningly said to Gopal, "You should be thankful to God that your lives have been saved. Had both of you not got down and instead continued to travel in that cart, nobody would have saved your lives. And you still wish to be in the cart. What made you think that?"

Gopal Bhand sorrowfully explained, "If both of us had remained in the cart, instead of deciding to get down, the resulting time delay could have been avoided and the rock could have fallen after the cart had passed.... and everybody could have been saved from such a painful tragedy."

Gopal's reply made everybody wonder about his selfless and noble thinking.

---

2. Maa Laxmi and Maa Durga are Hindu deities.

Popular Version

Systems, Contexts and Circumstances – these determine human thinking. All our thinking works either for good or bad. Positive thinking makes us stronger while negative thinking is exhausting. Great thoughts come from the heart and when reduced to practice, they become great acts. So make shift from negativism to positivism, from self-condemnation to self-elevation. Start thinking about the beautiful, pleasant and expansive nature of the mind.

Too Little, Too Late

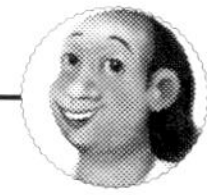

Fact of the Matter

True life is filled with insecurities, offering unknown surprises.

Fact Unfolded

Once, Raja Krishna Chandra Rai and Gopal Bhand happened to pass by the city graveyard. There both saw a *Sufi*[1] saint sitting in a corner who was probing some of the old skulls which lay scattered besides the graves with a long heavy stick.

'As real as it gets'

---

1. A Muslim sage who seeks direct experience of God.

The curious King halted near the saint. When the King enquired him the reason of spending time in the graveyard, the saint said, "People here are good friends," and continued to explain, "they do not backbite either. So I feel happy spending time here."

To this Gopal, who was just standing next to the King, asked, "O saint! But what are you doing here?"

"Oh, nothing very important," said the *Sufi*, "I am just trying to find out whether these skulls belong to Kings or paupers (poor and underprivileged people). But I find that they are all the same."

"And what is this long stick which you are having?" the King asked with surprise.

"Well, I'm measuring the earth," the saint replied. "Measuring the earth? What are your findings?" the King joked. "It is equal and the same, O King," the saint retorted. "Three arm lengths for me, in spite of my poverty and three arm lengths for you, in spite of your pomp and wealth."

The King gazed at Gopal with surprise and realised that the words of the *Sufi* alone are true.

Popular Version

A simple and most important factor is the fear of the unknown. Mostly, life is from the known to the unknown. Learn to love the unknown. The true focus of wise living is not to be limited to the known but to love the unknown. So, why worry about death when you have no time for life. Learn the secrets of living life wisely.

Tough Reality

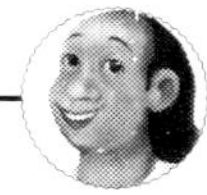

Fact of the Matter

Martin Luther King Jr rightly said, 'We have guided missiles, and misguided men.'

Fact Unfolded

As a routine affair, one late evening, Soumendra came to Gopal to have his hair cut. He comfortably occupied the chair to have his cut and soon entered into a good conversation with Gopal.

In the tête-à-tête that followed, both talked about so many

'Winds of Change'

subjects – from *Rajbari*[1] to the *Durga Puja*[2] and *Dhunuchi Naach*[3] and so on.

Suddenly, they touched the subject of God. Soumendra said, "Look Gopal, I don't believe that God exists in any form as you say so."

"Why do you say that?" asked Gopal curiously.

"Well, it's so easy; you just have to go out in the street to realise that God does not exist at all. Oh, tell me! If God ever existed, would there be so many sick people? Would there be discarded children? Would there be innocent children dying of hunger? If God existed, there would be neither misery nor pain. I can't think of a God who permits all these sorrowful things," answered Soumendra.

Gopal stopped for a while thinking but he didn't want to respond to Soumendra's opinion to prevent an unwarranted argument.

Gopal continued proficiently to finish his job. After the cut, both again started gossiping. Just as they stood chatting, they saw an old man in the street with long, cluttered hair and beard (it appeared that it had been a long time since he had his cut and looked so untidy and messy).

Seeing this, Gopal addressed to Soumendra, "You know what? Barbers do not exist at all."

"How come you say that barbers don't exist? Well Gopal, you're here. You are a fine barber in Nadia," Soumendra hurriedly spoke.

---

1. *The Royal Court/Palace.*
2. *Durga puja also referred to as Durgotsava is an annual Hindu festival that celebrates worshipping of the Hindu goddess Durga. Durga Puja is widely celebratedin the Indian states of Assam, Bihar, Jharkhand, Odisha, Tripura and West Bengal.*
3. *It is a dance done individually in front of the goddess during Durga Puja. It is performed in a circle with an earthen lamp-like base, inflamed with burning coals on top with incense sprinkled on the coals.*

"No!" Gopal exclaimed, "Barbers don't exist at all because if they did, there would be no people with long hair and beards like that old man who walks in the street."

"Ahhhhh, barbers do exist, what happens is that people do not go to barbers," clarified Soumendra.

"Exactly!" affirmed Gopal. "That's the point. Similarly, God does exist. What happens is that people don't go to Him and do not look for Him. That's why there's so much pain, suffering and discontent in the world. So, I always suggest everyone 'Turn to God. . . Before. . We return to God!!'"

The simple explanation of Gopal was enough to raise Soumendra's belief in God.

Popular Version

We see too little from a singular point of view. We are in fact victims of our limiting logic. When one views his thinking in its purest form; authentically and objectively sees one's thoughts and feelings through analytic identification; then truths are revealed; barriers break down.

Unlearn To Learn

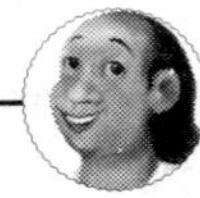

Fact of the Matter

We should act out of gratitude and be glad that we are in a position to be kind and make a difference to someone.

Fact Unfolded

One summer afternoon, while the King was returning from hunting, he felt terribly thirsty. On his way, he stopped at his jester Gopal's home for a glass of water to quench his thirst.

Gopal was delighted to see the King and welcomed him to his home. At Gopal's courtyard, the King saw a small orchard full of trees laden with pomegranate fruit. The neighbouring houses also had such similar orchards with the trees bearing a rich crop of pomegranates.

Gopal extended full courtesy to his royal guest. He immediately plucked the largest and reddest pomegranates from his orchard, and squeezed the juice from them. Then he gave the King a large glass full of rich, cool and refreshing juice.

The King delightfully took the glassful of juice from Gopal. The King looked around at the orchards as he sipped the juice, "Lovely trees," he said. "Do all of you make a lot of profit from the pomegranate crop?"

"A little," said Gopal softly.

'Masterstroke'

"How much do you pay by way of taxes?" asked the King curiously.

"Your Majesty is very kind," said Gopal. "There are no taxes on our fruit trees. There are taxes only on the grain we sell."

The King began to think that he should tax orchards as well as fields. With so many orchards in his Kingdom, there would be a welcome addition to the income of his Empire.

After a little while, the King again felt thirsty. He asked Gopal for another glass of juice. Gopal brought some pomegranates, but though he tried and tried, he could get no juice from them.

"I'm so sorry, Sire," he said. "These pomegranates refuse to give any juice. They are sensitive fruit. I think the trees have sensed that

Your Honour have an eye on them and intends to benefit himself. So they have dried up."

The King felt ashamed of his greedy scheme, and decided to forget about it.

Popular Version

If people could understand the beauty and pleasure of the law of giving, the world would be a wonderful and enjoyable place. Alas, such instances are few, and people in general apply profit and loss calculations; if they could leave it to the Cosmic Calculator and give with unconditional compassion, one would certainly receive more than one gives.

Spirit of Devotion

Fact of the Matter

Good people are all about clarity, consistency and credibility of acts.

Fact Unfolded

Captivated by the cleverness of Gopal Bhand, Raja Krishna Chandra had made him the *Khazanchi* – the Incharge of the Royal Treasury.

Although the envious courtiers could not tolerate this, the humble Gopal did his best to perform his duties.

'Knockout Blow'

Gopal being kind-hearted was always eager to help the poor and needy as a *Khazanchi*. He was regularly approached by poor villagers seeking financial assistance. After establishing their genuine needs, Gopal allowed cheap loans to the needy with the condition of 'repayment of the loans only on the death of the King'.

Such act of allowing loans to the poor made the people happy. But the condition of 'loan repayment on the death of the King' created an atmosphere of displeasure within the *Rajbari*[1]. The envious courtiers found this as a golden opportunity to instigate the King against Gopal.

Accordingly, they added fuel to the fire to raise the temper of Raja Krishna against Gopal.

Soon the King became infuriated when he came to know about Gopal's act of extending such conditional loans to the poor. The agitated King called Gopal to the *Rajbari* and shouted, "Gopal! What is this? This was not expected from you.! You are really a selfish person who is not fit for any reward. I have trusted you, but unfortunately you are anxiously waiting for me to die.... Unbelievable Gopal!"

Gopal just stood mute, observing the cunning smiles on the courtiers' faces. Gopal understood the malice of the jealous courtiers and after a while explained, "My Lord. . . I have been your loyal and will continue to be your faithful till my last breath. I granted loans to the poor only with a condition that the 'repayment of the loans will be only on the death of the King'. I know that these poor people would never have any amount of money to repay for their loans. Thus they will always pray to the Almighty that the King lives longer and never

---

1. The Royal Court/Palace.

dies, so that they can escape their liability to repay the loan amounts they owe to the Royal Treasury. I love my King, so I did such."

Listening to this, the King was taken aback and hurriedly stood to take Gopal in his arms with admiration. The courtiers just felt embarrassed.

Popular Version

We indulge in vices not only physically but more often – through our minds. Guard against this tendency. In haste, the King questioned the loyalty of his earnest jester.

Waste not, Want not

Fact of the Matter

We never know the worth of water till the well is dry. It is of no use to fill our pockets with money if we have got a hole in the corner.

Fact Unfolded

Raja Krishna Chandra Rai encouraged trade and he established numerous business centres to promote business. As a result,

'Money is round and rolls away'

relations with neighbouring countries prospered immensely. Even a merchant named Ananda Jayawardene visited Krishnanagar from *Ceylon*[1] to witness its flourishing trade and spent considerable periods in *Rajbari*[2].

After extending his Empire profusely, the King became extravagant and started spending wastefully on items of least importance. The King even ordered that entire Krishnanagar be given a new bright look by replacing all public ornamental items with new ones. This meant huge expenditure. The loyal jester Gopal Bhand became impatient at the King's weird moves of spending carelessly which was resulting into depletion of royal reserves. Worried, he thought of resolving the problem but could not find the way to do so.

The next day at *Rajbari*, when the King was busy deliberating trade affairs with Ananda Jayawardene, Gopal made a humble suggestion to the King to consider donating 1000 bed sheets to Buddhist *bhikshus*[3] of *arya-sangh*[4] who were on their noble visit to Krishnanagar.

Raja Krishna Chandra being a kind Ruler welcomed the suggestion and made immediate arrangements for the donation. When Gopal was just to take the King's leave, Jayawardene who was keenly observing the matchless generosity of the King, could not resist his anxiety. He requested Gopal to satisfy his curiosity and asked, "What will the docile *bhikshus* do with so many bed sheets at one time?"

---

1. *Present day republic of Sri Lanka lying on the southern Coast of Indian sub continent.*
2. *The Royal Court/Palace*
3. *Buddhist Monks who live a simple and meditative life. Generally, the Bhikshus live on donations.*
4. *Sangh is an assembly, company or community of monks with a common noble goal, vision or purpose.*

The clever Gopal pondered over Jayawardene's inquiry for a while. He perceived the situation to be an opportune moment to make the King realise about his extravagant and wasteful expenditure. So, Gopal immediately answered Jayawardane's question, "The *bhikshus* will replace old torn robes with new ones of those disciples who require replacement."

As expected, the question and answer session went a bit further.

"What will happen to the old torn robes of the disciples?" asked Jayawardene anxiously.

"The *bhikshus* will make small seating mats out of them," responded Gopal.

"What will the *bhikshus* do with the old seating mats?" queried Jayawardene.

"The *bhikshus* will segregate them and make pillow covers out of some of those," replied Gopal.

"Then what will happen to old pillow covers?" asked Jayawardene.

"The *bhikshus* will collect them to make dusting clothes or use them for filling mattresses," answered Gopal.

"Then what will the *bhikshus* do with the old mattresses and old dusting clothes?" asked Jayawardene promptly.

"They will make them into powder and mix them with the slurry for plastering walls," said Gopal satisfying Jayawardene completely with the resource management of the *sangh*.

Witnessing the session, the King also learnt a valuable lesson as was expected by Gopal and decided to implement the ideas of the Buddhist sangh into the governance of his own Kingdom's economy.

He immediately disbanded all wasteful activities announced by him and kept a strict vigil over all expenses thereafter.

Popular Version

Kingdoms fall...Empires crumble...Regimes collapse. It is the unwritten law of history. One who does not economise has to agonise. His reign falls from grace and comes to an end like this – so swiftly, so feebly, so abjectly. It is a basic rule not to waste anything, be it time or scraps of paper. Waste is worse than loss. So, one has to adopt judicious utilisation of available resources and needs to be careful of little expenses as a 'small leak can sink even a Titanic'.

Utterly Devoted

Fact of the Matter

Where there's a will, there's a way.

Fact Unfolded

Gopal Bhand had tremendous presence of mind which made him Raja Krishna Chandra's favourite court jester.

Gopal was poor and stayed in a shanty (hutment) which had a tattered roof and crumbling side walls. The straw on the roof was really thin.

'Full Coverage'

One wintry morning, Gopal eagerly gazed at the cloudy sky. There was a strong smell of rain in the air. The monsoons were to take off. Gopal plucked his brow and shifted his eyes on the torn roof. 'If it rained hard, the roof was bound to leak.' He thought gloomily.

Just then, Gopal's wife roared from inside the kitchen, "You're good for nothing! Have you cared to look at the roof of our house?"

"Hmmmm ... The straw is getting thin at places. The straw roof has to be redone from time to time. We need to put a fresh lot of hay to prevent leakage of rain water," clarified the worried Gopal.

"Despite that you are a courtier at the *Rajbari*[1], it is disgraceful that we still have straw roof to tend to," screamed the lady.

"This is our ancestral home and it just requires repairs," retorted Gopal.

"It's no use arguing with you," said Gopal's wife. "I just foresee that I'm fated to live in a straw hut all my life."

Gopal gave her a keen look. "There's something in what you say," he agreed.

The next morning, Gopal arrived quite late at the *Rajbari*. And came later and later each following day.

"What's the matter with you, Gopal?" asked the King intolerantly after a few days, "You always come late these days."

"Sire! I am just planning to have *Sravana puja*[2] at my place this year," said Gopal politely.

---

1. *The Royal Court/Palace.*
2. *Worship performed during the Bengali month of Sravana (mid-August) during the monsoons. It is considered to be an auspicious event.*

"Gopal, you have it every year.... I suppose," said the King anxiously.

"Yes, it's true. Well, it will be a special event this time, Sire," said Gopal. "I am planning to invite Your Majesty at my place that very evening of the *puja*."

"Very well, I'll be more than glad to be there," assured the King.

The day of *Sravana puja* arrived at long last. His wife was rather uneasy when she heard about the King visiting them.

"But where is the King going to sit? We don't even have a proper seat that is high enough for him!" she remarked in panic.

"You just leave the seating arrangements to me," countered Gopal. "Just tell me ... where's the ladder?" continued to ask Gopal.

"What do you require the ladder for? Dattey borrowed it yesterday," said Gopal's wife.

Dattey was Gopal's next-door neighbour. Gopal sped to his house.

"My best mattress is gone! It's not on my bed anymore," shouted Gopal's wife after a while.

"Don't scream, Lady. I've taken it!" explained Gopal.

"But why? Are you mad? First the ladder and now my mattress!" cried the lady in angst.

Right then, the King's men turned up to announce that he was on his way.

A while after, there came the sound of horses' hooves as the royal carriage rolled into the small lane. Gopal was at the door.

But instead of asking the royal party to step inside the angina[3] as usual, Gopal led them to the back of the house.

"Where are you taking us, Gopal?" asked the King in surprise. "This isn't the way to your house! Don't you usually feed people in your *angina*?"

"Of course not!" said Gopal, "I don't have a proper seat that's high enough for you in my house. I can't insult Your Majesty just because you have agreed to come. I have arranged for you to sit on my terrace – at least it's a place as high you're used to."

To the King's utter astonishment, Gopal pointed to the sloping straw-roof of his house. There was a mattress on it, hanging at an insecure angle. A ladder stood supported against the wall, barely touching the roof.

"There, Your Majesty," said Gopal in a modest voice, "a seat high enough, in keeping with your status."

"Are you crazy, Gopal?" shouted the King. "How can anyone sit on that sloping thin straw roof?"

"But Sire, I am not asking you to sit on the straw. I have spread a mattress for you to sit on," said Gopal. "It's quite easy to climb up this ladder. Only a few steps are missing."

"You must be mad if you expect me to go up that broken ladder and sit on your straw roof," cried the King. "I have never heard of such boldness!"

"It is not boldness, Sire," said Gopal, "It's the best I can do. How else can I entertain you in a mud house?"

---

3. Courtyard.

The King looked at Gopal, his ladder and the mattress hanging down. He burst out laughing. "I get your point," he said at last. "I'll send my masons the first thing tomorrow morning. They will convert your thatched hut into a fine brick house – a double-storeyed one! Satisfied?"

Gopal bowed low with folded hands well pleased with himself. But more than Gopal, his wife was happy.

Popular Version

Human reason needs only 'will' more strongly than fate because he who is of firm 'will' moulds the world to himself.

Wit and Wisdom

Fact of the Matter

A diplomatic move often serves one's purpose without making others annoyed.

Fact Unfolded

Gopal Bhand had a large appetite and was known to eat enormous quantities of food especially when invited to feasts.

One day, the *Zamindaar*[1] of Tehatta decided to test Gopal's eating capacity and thus invited him for lunch.

'Treating the Body Right'

1. *Zamindaars were an aristocratic and typically hereditary class who lived during pre-Independent India and held enormous tracts of land.*

Gopal happily accepted the invitation.

Next day, Gopal visited the *Zamindaar's* place for the lunch. Gopal ate everything offered to him – *Lebur Bhat, Luchi, Begun Pora, Jhaal Bhetki, Aloor Dum, Palong Shaker Raita* and *Sandesh*[2] with relish. Gopal ate as much as three men would have eaten and then emitted a loud belch.

The *Zamindaar* was astonished to notice Gopal's unmatched appetite.

"Enough?" asked the *Zamindaar* surprisingly.

"No place for even a single grain of rice more," said Gopal smilingly.

Just then a servant came in with a plate full of ripe mango slices.

"Mango!" exclaimed Gopal, his mouth watering. He took the plate from the servant and ate all the slices.

"Amazing," said the *Zamindaar*. "You said you did not have place for even a single grain of rice yet you consumed a plate full of mangoes. How do you explain that Gopal?"

"Very simple," said Gopal. "What happens when you walk into a crowded room? Everybody steps aside to let your royal person pass. Something similar happened here. The mango being the 'king of fruits', all the food in my stomach made way for it."

Saying this, Gopal walked away smilingly leaving the *Zamindaar* gazing.

---

2. *These are Bengali cuisines. Lebur Bhat is Lemon rice, Luchi is puri (fried bread), Begun Pora is roasted eggplant, Jhaal Bhetki is Bhetki fish curry in mustard, Aloor Dam is dry potato curry , Palong Shaker Raita is spinach raita and Sandesh is Bengali sweet dish.*

Popular Version

At times, politically correct statements work well. But we should not make a habit of using such unprocessed statements and dogmas as do our revered politicians.

❁❁❁

Wrong and Right

Fact of the Matter

The most successful people don't necessarily have the best of everything; they just make the most of everything they have.

Fact Unfolded

Like his father Raghuram Rai Raja Krishnachandra Rai was shrewd having political foresight. He had a number of courtiers to advice him in his daily affairs.

'Generous Dose of Positive Thought'

Hariram Tarkasiddhanta was a scholar who had joined the *Rajbari*[1] as a courtier at about the same time as did Gopal .

Years passed but Hariram did not acquire much importance and remained a menial, while Gopal was given reward after reward and promotion after promotion to become an admired dignitary.

Hariram felt that grave injustice was being done unto him.

So one day, while the King was leisurely taking a stroll in the royal garden, he very humbly said to the King, "My Lord, I have been faithfully serving Your Highness all these years. Gopal also joined at the same time. He is being rewarded regularly and being paid much higher than what I am getting. I pray Your Highness to also bestow upon me higher pay and rewards just like you do to Gopal."

"I will surely consider . . . You need not worry Hariram. Have patience," said the King politely.

Just then, a bullock cart passed across the Palace Gates. "You go and find out who is in that cart," the King hurriedly said to Hariram.

Hariram hurriedly went towards the Palace Gates, and came back soon. "They are Dhrupad and Kirti from Madurai and they also have a servant along with them, named Krishanu," Hariram answered.

"Go and ask them where are they going?" the King told Hariram.

Hariram went out again, asked them and returned. "They are going to Sagar Dwip," he informed the King.

"Go and ask why they are going to Sagar Dwip?" said the King.

So Hariram went again, and asked the strangers the reason for their travel. "We are going to attend a marriage ceremony and also

---

1. The Royal Court/Palace.

the *Gangasagar Mela*[2] on the occasion of *Makar Sankranti*," they informed Hariram. Hariram ran back and told the King what they had said.

The King said, "Find out whose marriage is it?"

Hariram went out again and returned after a while. "It is the marriage of the man's younger brother," he said.

"Go and ask when they will return," said the King.

Hariram went again, and came back. "They shall return next week," he said.

Gopal was away from the Palace at that time. He came to the King later. At that moment, another bullock cart was passing across the Palace Gates. The King asked Gopal to find out who were in the cart. He also called Hariram to his side, and asked him to remain nearby.

Gopal hurriedly went to the road, and returned in a couple of minutes.

"Who are they?" asked the King.

"May it please your Highness," said Gopal, "they are people from Lalbagh; they are two Muslims, one is named Aslam, and the other is his eldest son Ishfaq."

"Go and ask them where are they going?" said the King.

"That has also been asked, Your Highness. They said that they were going to Cooch Behar in North Bengal."

---

2. *The Gangasagar Mela is the largest fair of Bengal. It is a three-day event held in mid-January, on the occasion of Makar Sankranti, at Sagar Dwip when lakhs of pilgrims come for a holy dip at the confluence of the Ganga and the Bay of Bengal.*

"Go and find out why they are going to Cooch Behar," said His Highness.

"I have asked them that also. They have a property dispute for which they have to appear before the *Adhikari*[3] at Cooch Behar."

"Did you ask them what the case was?" asked the King.

"Yes, Your Highness. It is a case of division of Aslam's piece of land amongst his three sons."

The King turned to Hariram, and said, "Do you now see the difference between yourself and Gopal? You had to go five times to get all the information I wanted. Gopal went just once, and got even more information than you did."

Hariram bowed his head and agreed that the King was right to bestow respect and appreciation unto Gopal.

Popular Version

We are *karmayogis* as we have been given a body whose sole purpose is to perform actions perfectly. Focusing and emphasising on 'extraordinary in the ordinary' enhances core competencies and increases self-awareness for overall effectiveness. Have an attitude of 'I will better my best'. Then an unknown power in you will arise. So, there is a simple formula for living – get up in the morning and go to bed at night. In between, occupy yourself as best as you can. That way, we will be leading a far more sensible life.

---

3. Official deputed by the State to accomplish defined purposes relating to revenue, tax, law and order and so on.

Serious Approach

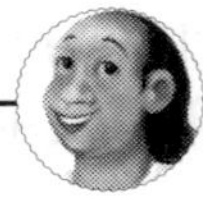

Fact of the Matter

It is 'Ethics', 'Tenacity', 'Rigour' and 'Analytics' that maketh a perfect man.

Fact Unfolded

Raja Krishna Chandra Rai patronised art and culture. Raygunakar Bharatchandra, one of the famous poets of the 18th century, was his

'Winning Trend'

court poet. Other men of letters at the *Rajbari*[1] included Ramprasad Sen, Pandit Baneswar Bidyalankar, Krishnananda Bachaspati, Jagannath Tarkapanchanan and Hariram Tarkasiddhanta.

Raja Krishna Chandra used to pose quick-witted questions to his courtiers to test their intellect.

Once, the King decided to check the aptitude of Gopal Bhand.

The King said, "Gopal, I want you to find answers to my three questions. These questions are:

(1) What is that which you give here and for which you receive a reward here?

(2) What is that which you give here but for which you receive a reward there?

(3) What is that for which you receive a reward neither here nor there?"

Gopal was bewildered to hear the King's peculiar questions. He thought intensely. After a while, Gopal said, "Sire! For answering your questions, I shall need seventy-five gold coins and a week's time. I shall provide answers to all the three questions." The King forthwith paid seventy-five coins to Gopal and waited anxiously for a week.

At the end of the week, Gopal returned to the *Rajbari* and said to the King, "Sire, I have found answers to your three questions. Allow me to present them."

The King agreed to Gopal's request. All the courtiers keenly awaited Gopal's answers to the questions.

---

1. The Royal Court/Palace

So Gopal explained, "From the seventy-five gold coins that you gave me, I deposited twenty-five coins with the *Zamindaar*[2]. It is credited to your account. You will receive an interest on the deposit. That is the reward that you will get. One has given it here and one will be rewarded for it here itself. Any time you want it, you will get it back with interest. This answers your first questions.

Your second question was, 'What is it that you give here and for which you are rewarded there?' Sire, out of the remaining fifty gold coins, I spent twenty-five coins to get food and clothing for the needy and the poor. And all this was done without you knowing about it. O King, you will be rewarded for this in the next world. That answers your second question."

Your third question was, 'What is it that you give here and for which you receive a reward neither here nor there?' Sire, now only twenty-five gold coins were left. Well, I spent these coins in vain pleasures – gambling, drinking, song and dance. For all that, you will be rewarded neither here nor there. I hope this answers all your questions, Sire."

Listening to Gopal's explanation, a wave of relief swept over the King and the onlookers in the *Rajbari*.

Popular Version

Make Self-Inquiry a Habit. You are always your own best *guru* (mentor), your own best teacher; the answers are always inside you.

---

2. *Zamindaars were an aristocratic and typically hereditary class who lived during pre-Independent India and held enormous tracts of land.*

Desire Again

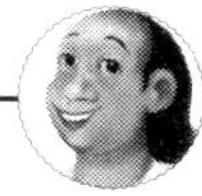

Fact of the Matter

To be fool is the gift of fate, but to play the fool to advantage, it is necessary to be a learned man.

Fact Unfolded

Once, Gopal Bhand visited a sweet shop famous for mouthwatering desserts – *sandesh*, *sarbhaja*, *sarpuria* and *rasgullas*[1]. At that time, the sweet shop was being manned by the *halwaikar's*[2] son aged around 8. Gopal took off his *chappal*[3] at the threshold of the shop

'Greed' and 'Need'

1. *Sandesh, Sarbhaja, sarpuria and rasgullas are some of the heritage foods of Bengal culture. These are sweet dishes and tasty desserts.*
2. *The main member who prepares dishes and manages the affairs of the shop.*
3. *Shoe*

and entered inside gleefully. Without seeking any permission, Gopal started picking and eating the sweets.

The little boy got irritated at Gopal's strange act and protested with annoyance. He asked Gopal's name impatiently, "May I know your name, Uncle?" Gopal replied in a friendly tone, "My child, your father knows me very well; my name is *Machi (housefly)*[4]."

The *halwaikar* who was relaxing lazily in the *angina*[5] of his house located at the backyard of the shop, hearing his son talking to somebody inquired, "My son! To whom are you talking?" To this, his son replied at once, "No one Father! It is *Machi* eating the sweets without seeking anybody's permission."

The *halwaikar* gulping another *paan*[6] replied, "My son, our sweet dishes are delicious. The *Machi* eats the sweets daily and it does not require anybody's permission for this. You need not worry. When the *Machi* is contended with its feast, it will go off on its own. So don't bother."

"Okay, Father!" the boy obeyed his father religiously and let the *Machi* (Gopal) eat the sweets patiently.

So Gopal ate all the sweets and left the shop contended.

Popular Version

There are layers of foolishness which engulfs a person. Such a person should be made to recognise and watch out for his foolish traits. To make the person (*halwaikar*) understand his foolishness is true awakening.

---

4. *The Indian housefly is called 'machi' in Northern and Western parts.*
5. *Court-yard.*
6. *The Paan is betel leaf containing flavored spices and mouth fresheners. The people in Northern part of India including Bengal savor paan after meals or otherwise.*

Hope Floats

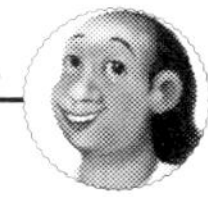

Fact of the Matter

Watch – The mystery of life is beyond our comprehension. We are mysteriously complete.

Fact Unfolded

Once after attending the *Vasantha Utsav*[1] in Birbhum, Gopal planned to visit Ranaghat.

So on his way to Ranaghat, he boarded a ferryboat to cross the mighty Jalangi River. The ferryboat was jam-packed with passengers

'Quick Fix'

1. *Vasanta Utsav is a fair celebrated in District of Birbhaum with the onset of Holi (March) to welcome the season of colours through songs and dances.*

who had just attended the *Utsav*. Though the ferryboat was bursting at its seams with passengers rubbing their shoulders with each other, Gopal managed to get a comfortable seat.

Draped in a silken *dhoti*[2], Gopal stretched himself on the seat cheerfully. While relaxing, he noticed his seat number to be 77 placed in the 7th row of the sitting arrangement. A while later, one of the boatmen charged Gopal 7 *cowries*[3] as fair for the journey and handed over to him a receipt token numbering 777. On reaching its destination, the ferryboat terminated at jetty number 7 where Gopal hired a horse-cart to reach the town. Gopal noticed the cart having its *pargana*[4] badge number as 7777. On reaching the town late in the evening, Gopal thought of staying in a lodge. At the lodge, he was allotted room number 77 located in the 7th block.

Noticing the recurrence of the number 7 at all occasions that day, the curious Gopal thought, 'There is something in all this.'

Ranaghat was famous for its horse races and people from far and wide visited the town to witness its horse races. Therefore, reading a message from fate, next day, Gopal keenly went to the race track and placed a heavy bet on the horse numbered 7.

Eagerly, he awaited the results of the race, almost certain that number 7 would work its magic. Well, it did in a big way. That horse ran with its full vigour in lane number 7 only to finish 7th to Gopal's great amazement.

---

2. Dhoti is a wrap round the waist. It is typical medieval Bengali male attire.

3. Cowrie (Kauri) is a glossy bright shell of any marine molluscs. It was used as money/currency in many parts of South Asia during ancient and medieval periods. It was the smallest unit of a coin in currency.

4. Pargana is province (territory) in which the Kingdom is divided for better administration. Each province (pargana) grants licenses (permissions) to the people to provide public services such as commutation etc.

Popular Version

The web of life is of mingled yarn. We cannot ascertain which way life would take us. At times all our expectations, plans, procedures and programmes turn out to be in vain. So, prepare the worst, expect the best and take what comes.

Leading the Way

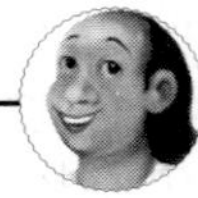

Fact of the Matter

When one is dishonest, look what price one has to pay for that!

Fact Unfolded

Kshitidhar, a simple trader of Krishnanagar, had to go on a long travel to attend the *Jalpesh Mela*[1]. So, he hid all his money (gold coins) in

'Tackling Vice'

1. *On the occasion of Sivaratri (February-March), a month-long fair is held at Jalpesh in Jalpaiguri. The fair centres round the age-old Siva temple dedicated to Lord Jalpeswara.*

a pot and put butter over it. In this way, nobody could see what was there under the butter in the pot.

Then he took the pot to his neighbour, the clever Dakshesh and pleaded, "Please keep this pot of butter for me till I come back." Dakshesh agreed to his request. Kshitidhar did not say anything about the money in the pot.

A month passed. Two months passed. But Kshitidhar did not come back. Dakshesh thought, 'I'm afraid the butter in the pot might have turned bad.'

And he took all the butter out of the pot and saw gold coins there to his great surprise.

Dakshesh's intentions turned evil after seeing the coins. He took the gold coins for himself and instead put many small stones into the pot in place of the coins. When Kshitidhar came back, he asked Dakshesh for the pot. Dakshesh gave the pot to Kshitidhar, who carried it home and took out all the butter. He wanted to take out the gold coins. But he found only many small stones under the butter.

He was very angry, but was helpless and felt distressed at his foolishness. How easily he had been made a fool? He thought day and night.

One day, while he was sitting perturbed with a gloomy face, his close friend, the razor-sharp Gopal Bhand, came to see him.

"You look sad, my friend! Why are you so sad?" asked Gopal.

"Oh, I am a silly man!" And he told Gopal the entire story about the pot of butter, the coins and the small stones.

“Well, I can show you how to get your money back. Let us go to the forest,” Gopal suggested.

And the two friends went to the close-by dense forest, caught a monkey there and brought it home.

“Now you go to your neighbour and say, ‘Please let your son come with me to the market. He can help me to carry food from the market,’” Gopal suggested to Kshitidhar.

Kshitidhar did so. Dakshesh sent his little son along with Kshitidhar. But they did not go to the market. Kshitidhar went home with Dakshesh’s son and locked the boy in his house.

Gopal said, “Now go to your neighbour with the monkey and say, ‘Here is your son.’”

Kshitidhar did so. At this, Dakshesh was very angry.

“Take the monkey away and bring back my son!” Dakshesh ordered Kshitidhar violently.

“Why, this is your son! If gold coins can turn into small stones, then why can’t a boy turn into a monkey?”

Dakshesh understood everything. He brought the gold coins to Kshitidhar who let the boy go back to his father.

Kshitidhar thanked Gopal very much. He wanted to give him a part of the coins, but Gopal did not take it.

“We are friends, aren’t we?” he said. “And friends always help each other, but never take money for that. Never, never!”

Popular Version

This is the time to stop, relax and just ponder . . . .!

'What are you in actual? A sieve or a winnow?'

Do you know the meaning of this?

'Be like a winnow (grain sorting pan) and not like a sieve!'

A sieve allows all the good stuff to pass through its pores while retaining the waste materials within. A winnow, on the other hand, discards the stones, chaff . . . , and retains only good grain. Just lean to be moral because morality is what moulds you.

❋❋❋

Preferred Choice

Fact of the Matter

We are so manipulative that we ourselves are not aware of our manipulations.

Fact Unfolded

One day, Gopal Bhand was lying leisurely on the beautiful beach of river Jalangi with his fishing pole held up in the sand and his solitary line cast out into the sparkling blue surf. He was enjoying the warmth

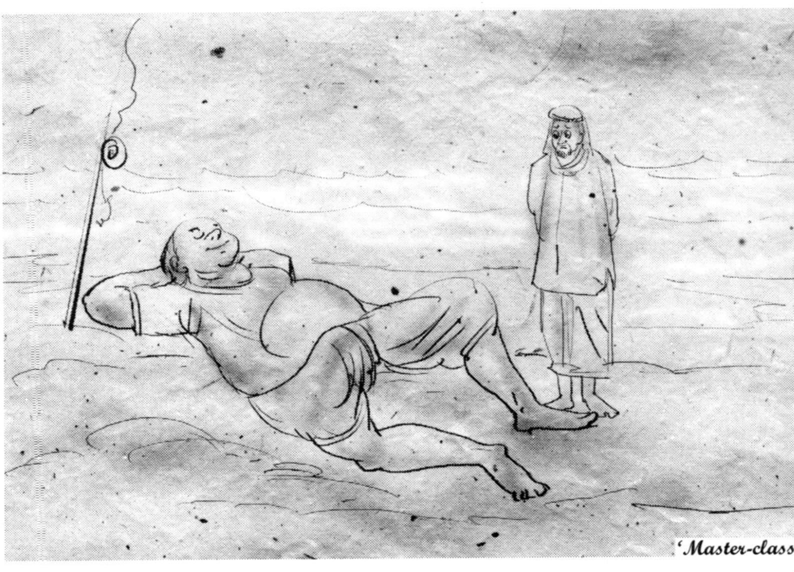

'Master-class'

of the afternoon sun and the prospect of catching a fish.

Just about then, a *Sheikh*[1] who was on his business visit to Nadia (Krishnanagar) from Persia came walking down the beach, trying to relieve himself of the stress of his workday. He noticed Gopal lying stretched on the beach restfully and decided to find out why this fisherman was resting instead of working harder to make a living for himself and his family.

"You aren't going to catch many fish that way! You are just wasting your precious time and energy," said the Sheikh to Gopal, "You have to support your family. So you should be working rather than lying on the beach leisurely!"

Gopal looked up at the *Sheikh*, smiled and replied, "Sire, in that case what will be my reward?"

"Well, if you work harder, you will be able to earn more to get bigger nets and catch more fish!" was the *Sheikh's* lucid answer.

"And then what will my reward be?" asked Gopal, still smiling.

The *Sheikh* replied, "You will make ample of money and you'll be able to buy a boat, which will then result in larger catches of fish of all varieties!"

"And then what will be my reward?" asked Gopal again.

The *Sheikh* was beginning to get a little irritated with Gopal's questions. "You can buy a bigger boat, and hire some people to work for you!" he said.

"And then what will my reward be?" repeated Gopal.

---

1. Sheikh or Shaykh is an honorific term in the Arabic language that literally means 'wise' or 'elder' or 'noble'.

The *Sheikh* got angry, "Don't you understand? You can build up a fleet of fishing boats, sail all over the world, and let all your employees catch fish for you!"

Once again Gopal asked, "And then what will be my reward?"

The *Sheikh* was red with rage and shouted at Gopal, "Don't you understand that you can become so rich that you will never have to work yourselves for your living again! You can spend all the rest of your days sitting relaxed on this beautiful beach, looking at the sunset. You won't have to care for anything in the world!"

Gopal, still smiling, looked up and said, "And what do you think I'm doing right now?"

The *Sheikh* was speechless at Gopal's reply. He just left the place without uttering another word.

Popular Version

Learn to enjoy little things; there are many of them. Enjoy yourself and enjoy today. Do not waste time by grieving over a bad yesterday. Who knows, tomorrow may not be as good as today. So shed your expectations before they become your primary source of grief and stress. You will feel lighter and happier.

Swinging Fortunes

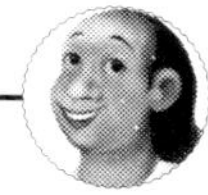

Fact of the Matter

The power of 'words' is immense. The only important thing is how we interpret 'words'.

Fact Unfolded

Bishwanath, the devout Brahmin from Ranaghat, decided to go on pilgrimage to *Kashi*[1]. Bishwanath's wife had died a few years ago, and there was no one to look after his two little children. So, he went to Bhudeb Bhashkar, the affluent village landlord for help...In front of

'Eyeing Full Control'

1. *Present day Varanasi situated on the banks of River Ganges. It is regarded as a pious city by the Hindus*

some villagers, he gave 1,000 gold coins to Bhudeb for safe custody for his children.

While giving 1,000 gold coins to Bhudeb, Bishwanath declared, "If I die during the journey, then you are my successor. In that case, whatever you want, you give to my children. And if I safely return, then I will take back all this deposit from you." Saying this, he departed for the pilgrimage.

Unfortunately, Bishwanath died on his way back from *Kashi.*

A few years after the demise of Bishwanath, when his sons reached their age of understanding, they went to Bhudeb and requested for the deposit which was entrusted to him by their father.

At this demand, Bhudeb felt irritated and said, "While going to *Kashi*, your father willed in front of the people that if he dies, I should give to you whatever I wanted. So I can give you only 100 gold coins."

At this, both the boys got annoyed and started yelling. Bhudeb called the witnesses and asked,"Do you people testify that the father of these boys gave me 1,000 gold coins that day when he was going to *Kashi* and while handing over the money to me, he also declared that, 'If I die on the way, then give my sons whatever you want.'"

All the witnesses testified that this was exactly what had happened that day when Biswanath handed the money to Bhudeb.

Therefore Bhudeb said to the helpless boys, "Now I won't give you more than 100 gold coins."

The poor children were perturbed and asked everyone for help. The people couldn't change this lawful trick.

Gopal Bhand somehow came to know about this incident. He

met the children and felt pity on them. In order to settle the issue, he took them and the witnesses to Bhudeb to inquire politely, "Bhudeb, why don't you give these orphans their lawful right?"

Bhudeb craftily said, "Gopal, while handing over 1,000 gold coins, their father willed that in case of his death, I should give them whatever I want, and therefore I won't give them more than 100 gold coins. Gopal . . . all these people are witness to this fact."

"O. . . . Bhudeb! Now, what you want is 900 gold coins, and according to your words, the deceased willed to give to his children whatever you want. Accordingly, give the children 900 gold coins that you yourself want. That is their lawful right," Gopal said softly.

Bhudeb became helpless at Gopal's answer and was compelled to give the orphans their lawful right of 900 gold coins. All those standing there felt happy at Gopal's wise decision.

Popular Version

Everybody can ague to attempt a solution to the problem. But to use the 'right words' at the 'right time' with the 'right person' in the 'right manner' for the 'right cause' to have the 'right effect' – that is the real wit. The goal in all areas of life should be able to make the right decisions and take the right actions naturally, without even having to think or strain.

Surprisingly Solid

Fact of the Matter

In order to be happy, one needs alertness to handle an opportunity.

Fact Unfolded

One fine day, the witty Gopal Bhand wrote a poem in praise of Raja Krishna Chandra Rai. The monarch was pleased with the poem and asked Gopal to name a reward which he would like to have.

'Innocence as a Prayer'

“Give me a dog of fine hunting breed,” demanded Gopal.

The courtiers looked at each other in disbelief. They felt Gopal had missed a golden opportunity to make some money and pitied him.

“If it is a dog you want, you’ve got it,” said the King.

“Your Majesty is generous,” said Gopal. “Now if I had a horse I could go hunting with the dog.”

“That’s not a big issue. You can have a horse too,’ said the King.

Gopal said, “I am grateful to you O King. But when I return from the hunt it would be nice if I had someone to cook the game I have brought.”

The King acceded and happily agreed to give him a cook.

“Your generosity is boundless,” said Gopal. ‘But where will I keep all these presents you have heaped on me? My house is meagre and could not accommodate the rewards which My Lord has bestowed upon me!”

The King understood and agreed to give him a much bigger house to live.

“I am overwhelmed,” said Gopal. “But how will I maintain such a large establishment, Your Majesty?”

“I will give you a coconut plantation,” immediately ordered the King. “It will fetch you enough to run a large household.”

“Never has the world known such generosity,” said Gopal politely, and kissed the King’s hand and left, leaving the courtiers speechless. Gopal tactfully managed to get everything from the King unhesitantly and without making anybody feel about his intentions.

Popular Version

Turn everything to your advantage without making anybody aware of your intentions. Handle the situation in such a way that it automatically pays dividends.

Supporting Role

Fact of the Matter

It is an equal failing to trust everybody and trust nobody.

Fact Unfolded

In a village on the outskirts of Krishnanagar, close to Gopal's house, there lived a poor man named Kunjabihari, who found it most difficult to make both ends meet. So he began to steal; and though he got plenty of money this way, he did not have peace of mind.

One day, the dejected Kunjabihari met Gopal and explained the commotion and unrest going on his mind. Gopal listened to him and

In a Tight Spot'

advised, "Kunjabihari! I know the hard-hitting circumstances you are facing. But, never speak an untruth in your life. If you speak only the truth and nothing else, God will always help you."

"But, Gopalji, I am a thief," Kunjabihari confessed, "how would I live if I start speaking the truth?"

"Don't worry about that!" answered Gopal. "Have faith in God, and still speak the truth."

With this Kunjabihari decided that he would only speak the truth, and nothing but the truth, from then on. That night, as usual, when he was on his way to commit one of his nightly robberies, Kunjabihari found himself confronted by a passerby.

"Who are you, and where are you going?" asked the passerby.

Kunjabihari was bewildered; he wondered how he could avoid answering this question. As he was determined to be honest, he replied, "I am on my way to steal, for I am a thief."

The passerby was amazed at this curious answer. He wondered what sort of a thief was this, who openly announced his intentions. So the passerby answered, "In that case, I will join you. We will equally share what we steal."

Kunjabihari was pleased and agreed to the passerby's suggestion. With the result, the two soon reached the King's Palace. Kunjabihari managed to get into the Palace, leaving his companion on guard at the door. With great difficulty, he next managed to break open a safe, in which he discovered three diamond-studded necklaces. Helping himself to two, Kunjabihari crept out and joined his companion.

As agreed, Kunjabihari handed over one necklace to his companion saying, "Brother, there were three necklaces in the safe, but to avoid any dispute between us, I stole only two. This one is therefore your share." And with that they parted company.

Next day, as usual, the Royal Court was held. In the Court, Raja Rai called his *Khazanchi*[1] and said to him sternly, "I understand that there was a theft in the Palace last night. Let me know what is missing."

The *Khazanchi* made a search, and soon came across the broken safe with the two missing diamond-studded necklaces. However, the *Khazanchi* was not an honest man. Thinking this to be an excellent chance to steal, he cautiously pocketed the third necklace.

Later he came before the King and reported, "*Sarkar*, three necklaces from a safe are missing! And nothing else."

But to his surprise the King shouted, "You rascal! You have stolen the third necklace. For only two were taken in the theft last night."

"But Sire!" stammered the *Khazanchi*, giving himself a way, "How do you know about that third necklace?"

"Because I was one of the two thieves who stole them," announced the King, to the *Khazanchi's* greater amazement.

Threatened with punishment, the *Khazanchi* now returned the necklace, upon which the King dismissed him at once. He sent for the honest thief and rewarded him suitably besides appointing him as an attendant in the *Rajbari*[2].

No doubt, Kunjabihari was amazed when he learnt the identity of his accomplice that night. But he was more astonished with Gopal's advice. From that day on, he was able to live a completely honest life.

---

1. Khazanchi is the Treasurer.
2. The Royal Court/Palace.

Popular Version

Wise Kings generally have wise counsellors but he must be a wise man himself capable of distinguishing one. And he should be competent to chew the cud of understanding appropriately to separate chaff from grain.

Helping Hand

Fact of the Matter

Let other's misunderstanding make you wise and not bitter.

Fact Unfolded

Gopal Bhand was in fact a very clever man. One day, as he was walking down the road, he met his friend Bishwanath returning from somewhere. He looked very sad, and in his hand he held the tail of a horse. "What is the matter?" Gopal asked Bishwanath.

'Pitching partnership prospering'

"My horse died in an accident. By the time I heard about it and reached the place, a fox had taken away the body and only the tail was left," Bishwanath replied.

Bishwanath was a poor farmer, and the horse had been his only expensive possession. Gopal felt sorry for him. "Give me the tail," Gopal told his friend, "I will get you a new horse."

Bishwanath had no idea how Gopal would produce a new horse using only a tail, but he knew how clever Gopal was, so he gave the tail to Gopal and went back to his farm.

Gopal walked down the forest path and saw a rabbit's burrow. He placed the horse's tail at the mouth of the burrow and sat down next to it, holding on to the tail. Soon a rich merchant passed by, riding a beautiful horse. He looked in amazement at Gopal sitting there holding the tail in his hands. "What are you doing?" he asked Gopal surprisingly.

"I was walking with my magic horse down this path when it ran into this burrow. You see, my magic horse can sense treasure and follow it anywhere. It has gone down the burrow to get the treasure and I am holding on to its tail. I will be rich when it comes out."

The silly merchant believed this story. Then Gopal said, "I don't have a bag to keep the treasure. Can you give me one?"

Quickly the merchant replied, "This bag of mine has a hole in it. Why don't you go back to your village and get a bag? I will hold on to the tail till you come back. Here, take my horse, that will be quicker."

Gopal left the place riding the horse after pretending great reluctance. The merchant eagerly waited for Gopal with the tail in his hand. An hour passed by, but there was no sign of Gopal, nor of the horse emerging from the burrow. The merchant was tired of waiting for Gopal and holding the tail. After a long wait, at last the merchant pulled the tail and fell back! When he peeped into the hole, of course he saw that there was nothing – no horse, no treasure, not even a rabbit! But Gopal succeeded in his plan of fetching a new horse for his friend.

Popular Version

Even out of unfavourable situations, good can come. Be more alert to think because thoughts can make you; thoughts can break you. By moving consciously and thinking appropriately, actions emerge. We need to deepen awareness to attract solutions to the situations we encounter.

In principle

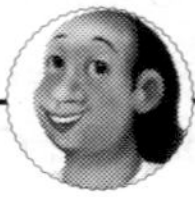

Fact of the Matter

Of all types of revenge, 'Tit for Tat' is the sweetest revenge.

Fact Unfolded

Once a beggar while passing through the market place in Krishnanagar, smelled the pleasing aroma of delicious, mouth-watering *sarbhaja* and *sarpuria*[1] sweet dishes. But the poor fellow didn't have any money to buy and taste them.

'Happy to help'

1. *Sarbhaja and sarpuria are some of the heritage foods of Bengal culture. These are sweet dishes and tasty desserts.*

Helplessly, he took out from his bag what he had – a piece of stale bread and softened it with the steam oozing out of the utensils placed at the fireplace in the corner of the sweet shop, and then quietly ate it.

The *halwaikar*[2] astonishingly watched this for a few moments. When his bread finished, the beggar wanted to leave. The *halwaikar* however unexpectedly stopped him to demand money. When the poor beggar denied paying anything, both of them exchanged hot words.

Incidentally, Gopal Bhand was passing by the market place. On seeing Gopal, the beggar requested him to decide the matter.

Gopal listened to the entire episode and said to the *halwaikar*, "Did this person eat any food from your shop or not?"

"He didn't eat the food, but he certainly benefited from its steam," said the *halwaikar* admittedly.

Gopal said to him, "This is correct. Listen!" He took a few coins out of his pocket, and showed them one by one to the *halwaikar*. After that, Gopal dropped the coins on the ground, and then picked them up. He said to the *halwaikar*, "Now take the noise of these coins."

Extremely surprised, the *halwaikar* asked, "What kind of way is this to give money?"

Gopal replied smilingly, "According to my opinion, the person that sells smells and steam should, in exchange, get the noise and tinkling of coins."

---

2. *The main member of staff who prepares dishes and manages the affairs of the shop.*

At this verdict of Gopal, everybody present there cheered while the *halwaikar* felt embarrassed. The poor beggar lauded Gopal to have saved him from the *halwaikar's* illogical demand.

Popular Version

If someone asks something for nothing; he should be given nothing for something. This is the principle of' 'Tit for Tat'.

Hack and Steal

Fact of the Matter

We can deceive some of the people all the time, and all of the people some of the time, but we can't deceive all of the people all the time.

Fact Unfolded

Gopal Bhand lived in a desolate house in Krishnanagar. Across it was a mean cobbler's shop which had a window opening towards his house.

Gopal had collected a few gold coins that he had hidden in the dirt in the corner of his house. Whenever he needed some, he would dug up the dirt and took out the needed coins, and buried the rest

'On vigil'

back again. As it so happened, one day when he needed some coins, he dug the earth but found that all of his money had disappeared. He immediately understood that the cunning cobbler, whose window faced his house, had taken the coins stealthily.

Without making any comment or commotion, Gopal went to the cobbler and patiently sat by him to chitchat. Gopal talked so much with him that the cobbler became confident and did not feel uneasy. He thought that Gopal knew nothing about the theft. Then Gopal said courteously, "My beloved friend! I have lot of wealth lying hidden at various places in the city. I will let you know of my entire hidden wealth. While I disclose you my wealth, please keep an account of all my money as I am weak in making calculations."

"Don't worry Gopal. . . You keep telling me and I'll keep adding your wealth," the cobbler said sneakily.

Gopal talked about some houses and buildings of the city, and with each he mentioned some coins lying hidden in those buildings. Then he told the cobbler that he had also buried certain amount of coins at a corner of the house where he is living presently.

When Gopal had finished his account, the cobbler added them all and said that there were a total of 2,000 gold coins.

Gopal thought for a while and said, "O friend! Now I want some advice from you."

"Okay! Speak," said the cobbler cleverly.

"I just want that all my money lying hidden at other places be buried at a single place in the house where I am presently living. In this way, I will keep my wealth safe from the thieves. What do you think of this idea?" Gopal explained innocently.

"Marvellous idea! Bring all the coins you have hidden at other places and bury them in your present house," suggested the cobbler excitedly.

"I agree to this. Now I should go and bring all the coins from other places to bury in this house of mine." Saying this, Gopal left the cobbler.

The cobbler thought to himself, 'I will bury back those coins which I have stolen. When Gopal brings the other coins and bury them, I will find and take all of them at once.' Thinking this, he buried back the stolen coins to their previous place at Gopal's house.

A few hours later, Gopal went to his house and examined the area where he had buried the money and to his astonishment saw that the cobbler had reburied the coins he had stolen. Gopal took out the coins, thanked God, left that house and went to another. The cobbler waited for a very long time for Gopal, but he was not to come back ever again. After much waiting, the cobbler finally understood that Gopal had tricked him, and so had got his money back cleverly.

Popular Version

Most of us are lazier in mind than in body. Change the mental recipe of thinking. It is not what we have that makes a difference, but how we use what we have that makes a difference. All of us are provided with beautiful minds but are we really making use of them? We have more than what we think we have. Discovering infinite resources for optimum usage makes us experience our life in a rich way.

Divine Presence

Fact of the Matter

Today, we have come to believe in the adage 'different strokes for different folks.'

Fact Unfolded

Nabadwip Dham[1], the birth place of Chaitanya Mahaprabhu, had traditionally been declared 'dry' (no alcohol sold). But, then a local

'Making his move'

1. Nabadwip is one of the most prominent pilgrimage destinations for Vaishnavas because it was here that Shri Chaitanya Mahaprabhu, the founder of Vaishnav religion and great social reformer were born and spent considerable period of his lifetime.

businessman decided to build a tavern (bar). A group of devout Brahmins from the *Sonar Gouranga Mandiram*[2] were concerned and planned an all-night prayer meeting to ask God to interfere.

It just so happened that shortly thereafter, lightening struck the tavern and burnt it to the ground. The owner of the tavern approached the *Rajbari*[3] and raised a claim against the temple, alleging that the prayers of the worshipping Brahmins were responsible for the loss. But the temple also deputed its most learned representative to argue in the *Rajbari* and upheld that they were not responsible for any such loss.

Next day, in the *Rajbari*, the King was baffled with the case being a peculiar of its kind. The perplexed King entrusted Gopal Bhand to preside over the case.

In order to settle the dispute, that very day Gopal went straight to the site and after his initial review, Gopal stated, "No matter how this case comes out, one thing is clear that the tavern owner strongly believes in prayer and the religious Brahmins do not. I am confused."

Popular Version

Attitudes, Styles and Responses of the people are 'traps' in today's turbulent times. We have to identify, strategise and practice 'trap-breaking' exercises to stay, fight and survive.

❁❁❁

2. *The Sonar Gouranga Mandiram is one of the most famous temples in Nabadwip. The temple has the Golden Shrine of Shri Chaitanya Mahaprabhu. His footwear has been kept here, in a glass case.*
3. *The Royal Court/Palace*

Dynamics of Business

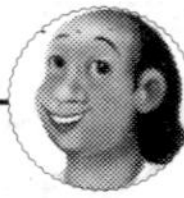

Fact of the Matter

What are the drivers of change? What are the new skills needed to face today's challenges? These questions in fact are required to be answered.

Fact Unfolded

In Krishnanagar where Gopal Bhand lived, there was a very miserly man named Ramendra. He would always try and find an excuse not to pay people for things that he bought from them. He would go to the city's hotel, eat some of the food that the waiter has served him,

'Speak Volumes, Words Optional'

and then he would get up and say, "I don't like the food. I am not going to pay for it." He would often go to the market to buy a few *ser*[1] of vegetables. He would then pick up a small portion of vegetables along with him leaving the remaining behind and tell the vegetable seller that he would pay only when the vegetables are delivered at his place.

Many people complained to Raja Krishna Chandra, asking him to punish Ramendra for his unusual and murky acts. As usual, Raja Krishna was baffled what to do, so he called his trusted jester, Gopal the barber and said, "Gopal! This miser is a very tricky fellow. You must do something to teach him a lesson."

So Gopal waited for the right opportunity to teach the miser a lesson. A week later he got that opportunity.

Ramendra decided to get a haircut. Since Gopal was a fine barber in Krishnanagar, he had to come to Gopal's shop.

Ramendra had already decided not to pay Gopal for the haircut. He said to Gopal, "I hear that you are an excellent barber in whole Nadia. I would like to challenge you to prove it to me. I want you to cut my hair so that every hair on my head is of the same length. If you do so, I will pay you handsomely."

Gopal knew that Ramendra was trying to trick him, so he listened carefully. Ramendra continued, "But remember, if even one hair is longer than the other, I will not pay you for the haircut."

Gopal accepted the challenge to cut Ramendra's hair. As a custom in Bengal, Gopal first applied oil on Ramendra's hair and massaged it well before the hair cut.

---

1. Ser is a measurement of weight. 1 ser = 930 gms (approx). The unit 'ser' was usually used during older periods.

As Gopal massaged his head, Ramendra felt relaxed and soon slept.

When he woke, Ramendra looked into the mirror and shouted out, "What! What have you done? You fool!"

Ramendra found that Gopal had shaved his head completely... Not a single strand of hair left on his head.

Gopal smiled and said, "You wanted me to cut your hair in such a way that every hair on you head was of the same size, well this is how I did it. This is the simplest way to do and there is no other way to do that Sire." Gopal continued to explain, "Now keep your promise and pay me good, or else I will report you to the King."

By that time a crowd had gathered to witness the event. Ramendra knew that he had been outwitted by clever Gopal. He had to pay Gopal the money, and from that day onward, he stopped indulging into miserly acts.

Popular Version

Quirky characters, lovable scoundrels and hollow movements are what predominant the current scenario. Today, when we live in uncertain times where nations can no longer operate as self-sufficient islands, there is an urgent need for 'change'. And everyone has to be a harbinger of this 'change'. A radical change in mindset, mode of knowledge delivery and assimilation seem to be the future road map.

End of Embargo

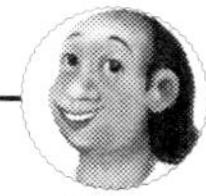

Fact of the Matter

'Tunnel vision' of having a narrow way of viewing the world predominates in most people. For such tunnel vision pessimists, life can be uncomfortable, if not intolerable.

Fact Unfolded

As a result of repeated *Bargi*[1] invasions of the Marathas, Raja Krishna Chandra Rai showed deep concern for improving the vigilance

'Challenging Tunnel Thinking'

---

1. *Bargi invasions took place almost as an annual event during Raja King Krishna Chandra's reign. Bargi invasions were conducted by armed Maratha horsemen in western Bengal and involved large scale plundering.*

of the Empire by his army. He made efforts to groom his troops to counter the Maratha attacks.

One day, the *Senapati*[2] assured the King that the troops were completely prepared and fully vigilant to counter any calamity.

At this, the King desired that the skills of the army be put to test. The King entrusted the job of this litmus test to Gopal Bhand.

The next day, Gopal disguised himself as a labourer of the *Rajbari*[3]. The Royal Guards stopped him just when he was walking out of the Palace gates pushing a wheelbarrow with a suspicious looking package in it. The guards opened the package and found it contained nothing but some old bits of rubbish, sawdust and floor-sweepings. They allowed Gopal to move out.

The next day, the Royal Guards stopped Gopal who was again pushing a wheelbarrow containing a suspicious looking package. Once more it contained nothing of any value.

The same thing happened for several days on the trot, until the Guards finally said, "Okay! We give up. We know you are up to something, but we just can't tell what. We promise not to arrest you, but put us out of our misery; please tell us what you are stealing?"

After thinking for a while, Gopal smiled and replied, "Wheelbarrows! I'm stealing wheelbarrows."

And saying this, Gopal revealed his identity and proved the King that their army still required more alertness and attentiveness.

---

2. The head of army
3. The Royal Court/Palace

Popular Version

These are the days of specialisation. Men have been trying to know more and more but still it proved to be less. This is to our advantage. In any case, the judges are always to be better. Remember, the centipede came by its name not because it had a hundred feet but because most men could not count beyond thirty when they came to name it.

Falling Flat

Fact of the Matter

A match between word and deed is indeed a virtue and such qualities should be inculcated in daily life.

Fact Unfolded

In Krishnanagar, there lived a cunning trader called Mukunda. Jaydeb, a simple merchant, was his friend. Over the time, Jaydeb had saved a lot of money.

'What's the Deal'

Jaydeb was keen to go on a pilgrimage to *Haridwar*[1], but he faced the problem of where to leave his precious savings. After giving a serious thought, Jaydeb came to Mukunda's shop and said, "Dear friend, I trust you more than anyone else in whole Krishnanagar. I am planning to go on a pilgrimage to *Haridwar*. Please look after my life's savings till I return from my pilgrimage."

Mukunda pretended to think seriously for some while and then said, "No Jaydeb. You know, money only spoils relationships. What if something happens to your money when you are not here? You will no longer be my friend."

As Jaydeb stood there thinking about this, Gopal Bhand entered the shop to buy some grocery. One of the boys helping Mukunda gave Gopal less change than he should have. Mukunda saw this and pretended to scold the boy, then ordered him to return the remaining money to Gopal and felt sorry to Gopal for such silly act of the boy.

Jaydeb, not knowing that this was just a pre-planned act put up by Mukunda to make him believe in his honesty, was convinced, "I have decided. I will leave the money only with you and none else."

Mukunda smiled, "Then let us do something. Let's take the bag containing the coins and bury it in an isolated place about which only you and I will know. That way, even if something happens to me when you are gone, you will know where your money is."

The innocent Jaydeb thought it to be a great idea. So the two went and hid the bag in a secret place. Jaydeb left for his pilgrimage the next day, happy with the thought that all his savings were in safe hands. After three months, Jaydeb returned from Haridwar. He dumped his luggage at home and went to dig out his bag. But even

---

1. Haridwar (presently in Uttarakhand) is an important pilgrimage city of the Hindus.

though he searched thoroughly, there was no sign of the bag anywhere.

In panic, he ran to Mukunda, who was busy in his shop. When Jaydeb asked him about the bag, Mukunda pretended to be surprised. "But I did not even go that way in all these months. Why don't you search for it again?" he said, putting on his most innocent look. Jaydeb had no choice but to believe him. Sadly, he made his way home.

On his way, Jaydeb met none else than Gopal, whom he had earlier seen at Mukunda's shop while offering his bag of coins to Mukunda for custody before going to *Haridwar*. Seeing his sad face, Gopal asked him what the matter was. Jaydeb told him the whole story. Gopal at once understood the crafty act of Mukunda. Gopal smiled and whispered a plan to him.

Not long after, Gopal came to Mukunda's shop, carrying a big box. "Brother, I have heard that you are a good and honest man. My nephew went on pilgrimage many months ago and has still not returned. I am worried and have decided to go and look for him. Will you look after my box containing five hundred gold coins while I am away?"

Mukunda could not believe his luck. He was about to launch into his idea about hiding the box, when an angry Jaydeb entered the shop and screamed, "Where is ..." But before Jaydeb could complete his sentence, Mukunda, afraid of being accused in front of Gopal, said quickly, "I forgot. I had seen some stray dogs digging around there and had removed the bag just to keep it safe. Here it is." And he handed Jaydeb the bag of money he had stolen many months back.

Now Gopal pretended he was seeing Jaydeb for the first time. "Brother, did you also go on a pilgrimage? Tell me, did you meet my nephew anywhere?"

Jaydeb, clutching his precious bag, said, "Yes, Sire. I met him at *Haridwar* a few days ago... He was on his way home. He should be here in a week or so."

Gopal leaned over and took his box away from Mukunda, "Thank you brother, you have saved me from an unnecessary trip. Now I will need some money to prepare for my nephew's welcome," Gopal added to Jaydeb.

And the two left the shop, holding their boxes. Mukunda could only stare at them open-mouthed.

Popular Version

Radical, Ethical and Authentic traits are required to be developed to succeed. False display and hypocrisy should not form a part of our nature. We never know when, where and by whom we will be tested for our conduct. To perform good actions should be the ideal state. After all, human beings are not born to be miserable.

Fatal Course

Fact of the Matter

A blow with a good analogy strikes deeper than a blow with sermons.

Fact Unfolded

Abanindranath, a rich Brahmin and a close friend of Gopal Bhand, lived in Birnagar. Abanindranath, though a devout Brahmin, fell in bad company and just spent his entire time in drinking. Such bad habit of drinking deteriorated his health and worsened his financial situation.

'All is well with innovative solutions'

Because of this, Abanindranath's helpless wife went to Gopal Bhand and requested him to interfere and make Abanindranath abstain from his bad habit.

The very next day, Gopal went straight to Abanindranath's house where he was busy drinking wine. Gopal sat close to him and explained that the consumption of wine is prohibited for a devoted Brahmin like Abanindranath.

But Abanindranath was adamant to quit drinking and wanted to prove that he was safe from the forbidden act of drinking, so he asked Gopal sarcastically, "Is it forbidden to eat grapes?"

"No!" said Gopal calmly.

"What if after eating grapes, water is drunk over them?" enquired Abanindranath.

"There is no harm," Gopal replied.

"After eating grapes and drinking water, what if one sits in the sun for a while?" quipped Abanindranath.

"Even then there is no harm," replied Gopal.

Then Abanindranath said, "Then if grapes and water are placed in the sun for a while, how does it become forbidden and prohibited?"

Gopal shook his head in agreement. After a while, Gopal smilingly asked Abanindranath, "Okay, tell me! If some dirt and mud is put on one's head, will it cause any harm?"

"No!" said Abanindranath instantly.

"Afterwards, if water is poured on it, will it cause any pain?" Gopal quipped.

"No!" again replied Abanindranath.

"If dirt, mud and water are mixed together and made to dry in the sun to form a brick, and thrown on a person's head, will it cause any pain?" enquired Gopal.

Abanindranath said, "True, the brick will break a person's head."

Gopal continued to explain, "The way dirt, mud and water mixed together dried as a brick break a person's head and cause him acute pain; likewise, grapes and water mixed together and placed in the sun become a thing that the Hindu law declares it as impure and forbids its intake by a devout Brahmin. Drinking wine causes the person and his near and dear ones many troubles and it becomes obligatory to punish its drinker."

Hearing the justified statement of Gopal, Abanindranath was distressed and felt sorry for his conduct. He decided never to consume wine thereafter.

Popular Version

The only thing to influence people is through sound examples. An example speaks loads.

When Benjamin Franklin wished to interest the people of Philadelphia in street lighting, he didn't try to persuade them by talking about it – instead he hung a beautiful lantern on a long bracket before his own door. Then he kept the glass brightly polished, and religiously lit the wick every evening at the approach of dusk.

People wandering about on the dark streets saw Franklin's light a long way off and came under the influence of its friendly glow with grateful hearts. To each one it seemed to say: "Come along! Here is a safe place to walk. See that cobblestone sticking up?

Don't stumble over it! Good-bye! I shall be here to help you again tomorrow night, if you should come this way."

It wasn't long before Franklin's neighbours began placing lights in brackets before their homes, and soon the entire city awoke to the value of street lighting and took up the matter with interest and enthusiasm.

Fuel for Thought

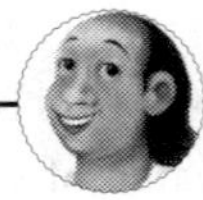

Fact of the Matter

One of the greatest paradoxes of life is one's failure to understand and unfold the truth in existence.

Fact Unfolded

In Krishnanagar there lived a merchant who had a small grocery shop and a young son named Devabrata. Devabrata was gentle and loving, but he often did not know the right thing to do. The merchant always worried about what would happen to the simple boy when he died.

'The Son' shine'

One day, the merchant called Devabrata to him and said, "I am getting old, son. When I die, I will leave you the shop, but you will have to work very hard to earn enough. I want you to promise me three things, which will make sure that you live a happy and prosperous life."

"I promise," said Devabrata. "Tell me what I have to do."

"Firstly, do not walk in the sunshine from your house to the shop," said the old merchant, "Secondly, let rice be your daily food. And, last of all, marry a new wife every week," the merchant continued to explain Devabrata.

Devabrata obediently promised his father to do all three, but he was very puzzled. "What do you mean, father?" he asked, "I shall do what you say, but I do not understand how it will help me?"

"Never mind," said the merchant. "In time, you will understand everything."

Soon after the merchant died. Devabrata remembered his promises, but wondered what to do.

The first promise was 'do not walk in the sunshine.' Devabrata was puzzled over what to do. He just decided to build a shelter over the road from his home to the shop. It was a costly project and everybody began to make fun of Devabrata for spending his inheritance in this way.

Devabrata was upset when people laughed at him, but he was determined to do as he had promised. The second promise 'let rice be your daily food' was easy enough to follow, though it soon became rather dull.

The third piece of advice was the worst of all. No girl would agree to marry him for only a week. The entire town came to know about Devabrata's promises. He became the laughing stock of the whole town.

One day, a young girl called Deeptimoy heard the story of Devabrata. She felt sorry for Devabrata but also admired him for trying to do what he felt to be his duty. She secretly met Devabrata at the shop and became impressed with his innocence and commitment. She gathered courage and told her family that she would marry Devabrata.

Her family was horrified at the girl's foolish decision. When the girl became adamant to marry Devabrata only, her father went to his close friend Gopal Bhand for advice. Gopal heard the entire episode and assured to tackle the problem soon.

Next day, Gopal visited Deeptimoy's house. The family of the girl cried, "Deeptimoy is just acting childish Gopal! What will she do when Devabrata sends her away after a week?"

"He won't," said Gopal confidently. "You'll see! Just allow her to marry Devabrata. Have faith in me," Gopal continued to give assurance to the family.

The family had no other alternative, but to agree to Deeptimoy's wish.

Next day, both Devabrata and Deeptimoy met each other. Devabrata liked Deeptimoy for she was both beautiful and charming. Being a good man, he began to tell Deeptimoy's family of his promises. But Gopal said, "We all know about it. Do not worry."

They had a grand wedding. There were coloured lights, music and lots of good things to eat. There were many guests who enjoyed themselves. But that did not stop them from saying, "How silly the whole affair is. The young wife will have to leave in a week."

The week passed too quickly. On the seventh day, Devabrata woke up feeling miserable. 'Today I will have to send Deeptimoy away,' he said to himself.

All day long, Devabrata was miserable. Finally, in the evening, Gopal came to their house. While Gopal sat patiently, Devabrata told Deeptimoy, "You know what I promised my father. You have to go away."

"You are a foolish fellow," said Gopal. "Your father was wise and kind. Do you think he would really tell you to do things that would make you the laughing stock of the whole town?" Gopal continued to tell Devabrata.

"Then, what did he mean by his three strange promises?" asked Devabrata surprisingly.

"When your father said that you should never walk in the sunshine from your house to the shop, he meant that you should go to the shop early in the morning, return late and work at your business all day. When he told you to eat rice, he simply meant you should eat what was necessary and not be extravagant," explained Gopal.

Gopal's explanation surprised Devabrata.

"But the third wish!" cried Devabrata in utter astonishment, "That can only mean what it says. Marry a new wife every week."

"No," said Gopal, "your wise father meant that you should always treat your wife lovingly. If you always welcomed her with the same love as you did when you were first married, she would be like a new wife to you each week," Gopal explained softly to end the long lasting dilemma.

Devabrata and Deeptimoy were amazed with Gopal's wisdom.

So was Deeptimoy's family. They loved the couple all the more and blessed them with long life.

Popular Version

We often fail to see the truth due to our ignorance. We are ready to go to the Moon and the Mars, but are foolish to unfold the truth in existence. This is the power of ignorance. Ignorance has its own delusive power. Thus, make it a habit to realise the truth in existence. Let us have a deep commitment to know the truth. Let it be the seed from which understanding emerges. And let us open wide the windows of wisdom.

Gallant Effort

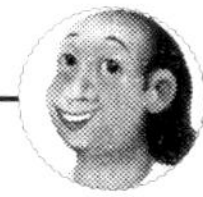

Fact of the Matter

Greed is an unwise way of making life meaningful.

Fact Unfolded

Deependu was a cunning merchant in Krishnanagar. He was ready to do anything to earn money. No one knew what trick he would be up to next.

Gopal Bhand was witty but a simple village man. Once, an affluent landlord gifted a beautiful white horse to Gopal for his

'Surprisingly Solid'

unmatched intelligence. Soon Gopal started loving the horse more than anything else. Everyone in the village knew about him and the horse. Gopal usually narrated heroic incidents about his horse to the neighbourhood children who felt thrilled listening to such happenings.

But the crafty Deependu had his evil eye on the horse since long and was always trying to think of a way to get it for himself.

One day, Gopal rode his horse to the *Gangasagar Mela*[1]. On his way back, he met Deependu. The sneaky merchant thought, 'Gopal is a simpleton. Let me see if I can trick him out of his horse.'

So he said to Gopal, "You are a poor fellow Gopal, and you have a family to feed. How do you manage? You must always be in great need of money. I have an idea. What does a young man like you need a horse for? Sell it to me and I'll make you rich in return."

Gopal replied, "No, I don't want to sell the horse."

But Deependu was not one to give up so easily. He followed Gopal, offering him more and more money. Finally, when the offer reached 500 gold coins, Gopal paused and seemed to give it a thought. Then he said, "Five hundred gold coins seem like a good price. But I have a condition. If you agree to that, I will give you my horse."

By now Deependu would have agreed to anything. "What is it? Tell me," he said impatiently. Gopal said, "You must give me the entire money right now, and I will give you the horse only when I have given you ten lashes."

"That's all!" exclaimed Deependu breathlessly. Ten lashes was nothing for Deependu. He would resell the horse for over 1000 gold

---

1. *Gangasagar Mela is the largest fair of Bengal. It is a three-day event held in mid-January, on the occasion of Makar Sankranti. Lakhs of pilgrims come for a holy dip at the confluence of Ganga and the Bay of Bengal.*

coins in the market. He was even ready to take twenty lashes to make such a profit. He agreed instantly. Then he ran home and got the money for Gopal. He also brought a whip for Gopal to lash him with. Gopal counted the coins carefully. Then he took the whip. One, two, three .... the lashes fell on Deependu's back in quick succession. By the eighth lash Deependu was ready to cry, but he told himself, only two more and the horse would be his. He had dreamt of buying it for so long.

Nine. . . . Deependu waited, holding his breath for the last and final lash. But what was this! Gopal had mounted his horse and was riding off, merrily throwing the whip on the ground!

"Wait!" shouted Deependu in anger, "What about the tenth lash? And where are you taking the horse? We had a deal."

Gopal stopped and said, "I agreed to give you the horse only after I have given you ten lashes. Now I don't feel like giving you the last one. It upsets my dear horse. I'll give it to you only when I am in the mood. Till then, goodbye!"

"Come back, you cheat!" screamed Deependu. He cried and complained to the crowd that had gathered. But the crowd that gathered around him also agreed. A deal was a deal after all. Gopal could give the tenth and final lash to Deependu whenever he wanted, and till then the horse could not belong to Deependu.

Gopal rode away, richer by 500 gold coins. Deependu waited for many, many days for the whip to fall on his back finally. Of course, it never came!

Popular Version

Greed means a desire for more without seeing the richness of what you already have. An action born out of greed deepens your ignorance. Greed enhances quantity and not quality. The beauty of life has never been in quantity but in quality. Hence, in India even a King bows down to a monk who has not quantity but quality. So be grateful for what you have and not sad for what you don't have.

Rare
Insight

Fact of the Matter

Sharp pencils make clear lines. Similarly, a sharp mind makes better decisions and not bitter decisions.

Fact Unfolded

Two travellers namely Keshab and Paban were on their way to Krishnanagar. Midway of their journey, they sat together to have their meal at a convenient spot nearby a flowing stream. When they opened their food packages, they noticed that Keshab had 5 loaves of bread while Paban had just 3.

'Through the looking glass'

As they were about to begin their meal, a third traveller named Somnath who was passing by, queried whether he should also join them to share their meal. At his request, both Keshab and Paban happily agreed Somnath to join them.

The three travellers had a pleasant time together. They cut each loaf of bread in 3 equal parts to share the food equally amongst them. Each of them ate 8 broken pieces of the loaves.

At the time of leaving, Somnath took out 8 gold coins and gave to Keshab and Paban and asked them to divide the coins between themselves. After giving the coins, Somnath went away.

On receiving the coins, Keshab and Paban started quarrelling as to who should have how much of the coins.

A disagreement arose between them on the matter of distribution of the gold coins. Keshab who had 5 loaves demanded 5 gold coins, while Paban who had 3 loaves insisted on dividing the money in two equal parts. It was a question of principle and none was ready to forego his right.

The dispute intensified. Since there was no amicable solution, both agreed to approach the *Rajbari*[1] for settlement.

The dispute was finally brought to the *Rajbari*. After listening to the dispute, Raja Krishna Chandra Rai desired Gopal Bhand to decide the matter.

Gopal attentively listened to the account of Keshab and Paban. After thinking for a while, Gopal addressed to Paban, the three-loaf-man, "Brother! Just accept the 3 gold coins which your companion offers you, for, in reality, you don't have a right to even those 3 coins."

---

1. The Royal Court/Palace

But Paban was adamant to take only an equal share of 4 gold coins and nothing less. He exclaimed, "It is not only the money for which I'm arguing; it is my right that I should get. If it is proved beyond doubt that I do not deserve an equal share of gold coins, I will have no complaint."

At this Gopal explained, "Well, then listen! You will have just 1 coin," Gopal continued. "Both of you had a total of 8 loaves between yourselves. Each loaf was broken in 3 parts to share the food equally. Therefore, there were 24 equal parts and each of you ate 8 broken pieces of the loaves. Your 3 loaves made 9 parts out of which you have eaten 8 portions, leaving just 1 to the third traveller. Your friend Keshab had 5 loaves which when divided into 3 each made 15 pieces. He ate 8 pieces and gave 7 pieces to the guest. As such the guest shared 1 part from your loaves and 7 from those of your friend Keshab. So you should get only 1 gold coin and your friend should receive the remaining 7 gold coins."

And with this just verdict, the Court cheered at Gopal's wit leaving Paban open-mouthed.

Popular Version

Every day is a new quest, a new adventure, a new challenge. Be sharp to see the whole picture. We are usually victims of our petty needs. One of the greatest needs is to investigate our needs thoroughly and wisely. One has to be a Columbus to see life's hidden agenda.

Steve Jobs, co-founder of the Apple Inc., preoccupied himself to find life's higher purpose through his imaginative leaps that were instructive, unexpected and at times magical. So one needs to be a pathfinder to absorb information, sniff the winds and sense what lies ahead.

Sigh of Relief

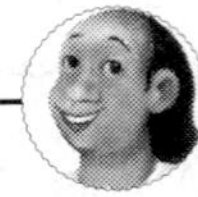

Fact of the Matter

Wisdom lies in close analysis of the situation to make a choice wisely.

Fact Unfolded

Once a man was caught stealing a bag of onions and was taken before the King in the *Rajbari*[1] for punishment.

The King desired Gopal Bhand to decide the punishment for the thief.

'Images to the Rescue'

1. *The Royal Court.*

Gopal gave the thief a choice of three punishments, "You can choose any one punishment. Either you eat all the onions you had stolen at one sitting or submit to a hundred lashes of the whip or pay a fine."

After thinking for a while, the thief said that he would eat all the onions. Gopal agreed to the thief's choice of punishment. He began confidently enough but after eating a few, his eyes began to burn, his nose started running and his mouth felt as if it were on fire.

"I can't eat the onions," he said, "give me the lashes instead."

Gopal agreed to give the thief a hundred lashes. But after he had received a few strokes, he began to turn and twist to avoid the whip.

"I can't bear it!" he screamed, finally, "I'll pay the fine."

Gopal agreed to the thief's wish. So the thief paid the fine and was let off, but he became the laughing stock of the entire city for having taken three punishments for the same crime.

Popular Version

Most of us are living an unconscious and unaware life and thus lack clarity. With unawareness, we experience moments of confusion leading to indecisiveness. This creates absurdity. So, what is required is proper scanning of the environment to have power of clarity.

Some Respite

Fact of the Matter

To look is one thing; to see what you look at is another; to understand what you see is a third; to learn from what you understand is still something else; but to act on what you learn is all that really matters.

Fact Unfolded

Raja Krishna Chandra Rai, the brave son of Raghuram Rai, always took concerted efforts to uplift the Hindu Rule amidst the Muslim power.

During his rule, there was political turmoil and instability in Bengal. The Nawabs became independent governors. And the King

'Sweet Secrets'

had to face revolt from these Nawabs – mainly from Siraj-ud-Daula and *Mir Qasim*[1] apart from Marathas.

Raja Krishna had to even move his capital to Shivnivash for protection against the Marathas. Not only this, he had to collaborate with *Robert Clive*[2] against the Nawabs to hasten their downfall.

In short, the King was totally dejected with the sad political affairs of his Empire.

Once, for a change from his monotonous routine, the King decided to undertake a brief visit of the city. Accordingly, the King and his favourite jester Gopal, disguised themselves as ordinary peasants and visited a crowded market of the city.

While crossing the market, Gopal noticed a poor old lady with a bucket full of fish putting a board reading *'Fresh Fish Sold Here!'* at a place by the side of a compound.

Standing back, the lady viewed her own handwork, checked if everything was okay. The lady read what she wrote on the board, once again. After a while, she again read the board .. .and again...

Gopal continued to observe the lady's strange behaviour. A little later, the King and Gopal saw the lady mounting a ladder supported against the wall to erase the word 'fresh' from the board. After reading the board carefully and thinking for a couple of minutes, the lady again climbed the ladder to erase the word 'sold' from the board.

---

1. *Chief political rivals of Raja Rai.*
2. *Major-General Robert Clive also known as Clive of India, was a British officer who established military and political supremacy of East India Company in Bengal. Together with Warren Hastings, he was one of the key figures in the creation of British India.Raja Krishna Chandra collaborated with Robert Clive, thus hasteningthe down fall of Siraj-ud-Daula the last independent Nawab of Bengal, Bihar and Odisha..*

After reading watchfully, the lady again scaled the ladder to wipe out the word 'here' from the board. A couple of minutes later, she again ascended the ladder to wipe out the word 'fish' and leave the board bare and empty.

A few hours rolled by. Gopal and the King stood there watching the proceedings of the lady thoroughly.

Gopal, unable to control his anxiety, walked towards the lady who was busy with her thoughts. The King followed Gopal.

After an exchange of smile, Gopal asked the lady the reason for her peculiar act of wiping off the words from the board one after the other.

The lady initially hesitated a bit but continued to explain, "Sire, I am a poor old widow. I have visited this market for the first time to sell fish. I put a board reading *'Fresh Fish Sold Here!'* Now, after reading the board carefully, I doubted 'would anyone sell stale fish?' Then why to use the word 'fresh'? So, I erased the word 'fresh'. The board read *'Fish Sold Here!'*

When I saw the signboard again, I wondered 'have I brought the fish to donate?' It is well understood that I am going to sell it... so I thought the word 'sold' is unnecessary.' Thus, I wiped out that word too. Now the signboard showed *'Fish Here.'* After seeing the signboard, I laughed. It was obvious that the fish was here and not somewhere else! So why the word 'Here'? And I removed that word also," saying this, she grinned.

After a brief pause, the lady further clarified, "Now all that remained on the signboard was the word *'Fish!'*. Finally, I saw the signboard and thought, 'anyone who comes to the market can identify by the very smell of fresh fish. As soon as they see the fish, they would recognise it! There was no doubt about that! Then why at all the word 'Fish'?' So I erased the word 'Fish'! Now the signboard is left bare and empty!" Explaining this, the lady walked off to attend to her chores.

Gopal stood silent for a while. Gopal and the King looked at each other for some time without speaking. The King, however, was confused.

Gopal clicked his tongue, chuckled and said to the King softly, "Sire! This is in fact the paradox of life. All our problems are like that signboard of the lady. Once we learn to view the problems in the right perspective, our problems too would disappear. But the saddest part here is that we do not know how to view things!"

The King shook his head slowly and with a solemn face warmly passed a look at Gopal. Listening to Gopal, the King felt relieved of his agony with his face lightened up.

Popular Version

What are the things necessary for seeing? Is it sufficient to have eyes? 'No, eyes alone are not enough, one must have awareness,' says Lord Krishna in the *Shrimad Bhagavad Gita.* Only when we have awareness, shall we know to discern the difference between things, people and ourselves. Lord Krishna has further expounded in the *Shrimad Bhagavad Gita,* 'Learn to view equally both sorrow and joy; be open to joy, be open to sorrow. They are the two sides of the same coin. Try to learn from both ... clarity will emerge. This clarity will bring you bliss!'

Speed of Thought

Fact of the Matter

If we really crave to cry out 'Eureka', let our thinking be inclusive and not exclusive.

Fact Unfolded

Gopal Bhand was a clever barber and everybody in Krishnanagar knew about this fact. One day, he learnt that Raja Krishna Chandra Rai along with *Robert Clive*[1] would be stopping for a night in the

'Heartiest Felicitations'

1. *Major-General Robert Clive also known as Clive of India, was a British officer who established the military and political supremacy of the East India Company in Bengal. Together with Warren Hastings he was one of the key figures in the creation of British India. Raja Krishna Chandra collaborated with Robert Clive, thus hastening the fall of Siraj ud-Daulah the last independent Nawab of Bengal, Bihar and Odisha.*

village on the outskirts of Krishnanagar. He decided to give a gift to the King and perhaps earn a small reward. He took his best cock to the King and presented it to him.

The King was very pleased to get such a fine bird. When Clive enquired the King about Gopal, the King explained him about Gopal's wit. *Robert Clive* too noticed the intelligent look on Gopal's face and requested the King to put Gopal to a test. The King agreed to Clive's request and asked Gopal, "In my family, I have a wife, two sons and two daughters, and you are my guest today. Tell me, how can I divide this cock rationally among these seven people?"

Gopal thought for a while and said, "It is easy. You are the head of the family, so you should get the cock's head. Your wife will get the cock's back as she is the backbone of the family. Your daughters will one day get married and go away, so they should get the two wings, and your sons will follow the path you show them, so they should get the legs."

"And what about you?" the King asked.

"I am the guest, so I should get whatever is left over," answered Gopal.

The King and Robert Clive were pleased by this reasoned and rational answer and presented Gopal with a gold coin.

Now Gopal had a foolish neighbour, Basant, who became very jealous when he heard about the reward. Basant too decided to present the King with not just one but five cocks to earn himself five gold coins.

Later that night, Basant also appeared before the King with five fine cocks. Basant introduced himself to the King and pretended to be wiser than Gopal. When he gifted the cocks, the King eagerly asked him the same question, "In my family, I have a wife, two sons and two daughters, and you are my guest today. How can these five cocks be divided rationally among these seven people?"

Basant was dumbstruck. Who knew the King would ask such a difficult question? As he stood trying to calculate, the King sent for Gopal.

Gopal heard the question and quickly worked out the answer, "Now, there are 5 cocks and 7 pupils – the King, the Queen, two princesses, two princes and a guest, that is, there are total 12 in number. We will divide everyone into groups of three," he said smilingly. "Your Majesty and the Queen will get one cock. The two princesses and one cock will be another group. The two princes and one cock will form the third group. I will form the last group with the remaining two cocks, so I will get two cocks."

The King smiled delightedly at this answer so did Robert Clive. Not only did the King rewarded Gopal but Robert Clive also presented Gopal with ten gold coins. The King turned to Basant who stood there open-mouthed, still counting on his fingers. "The coins are rewards for Gopal's intelligence, not for the cocks," the King explained gently and laughed heartily.

Popular Version

Success depends on the ability to covert unfavourable circumstances into favourable ones through wise thinking. The art of wise thinking is deepening our awareness into our unawareness and see how we mentally rehearse our problems in our mind. A thinker always asks a question ... the 'why' of things. Why is the sky blue? Why are the leaves green? This causes great things to emerge from small acts. Let wise thinking be a way of life.

Chasing Wisdom

Fact of the Matter

Don't follow the grapevine (rumour). Rather choose thoughts to know the facts and situations thoroughly.

Fact Unfolded

Gopal Bhand lived with his wife in Krishnanagar. Though a poor couple and barely having enough to live on, Gopal was good and pious.

Gopal had one habit which always annoyed his wife. He was

'Costly Mistake'

always inviting people he met to his home for a meal when there was hardly enough for the two of them. 'And it's not as if he invites people we know,' she thought angrily. 'Strange men he has rarely met before – who knows what kind of people they are! And he gives away anything they say they need – clothes, food, vessels.' But her husband never listened to her protests.

One day, Gopal's wife decided that this nonsense had gone on long enough. So the next time her husband brought some stranger home for a meal, she resolved to teach him a lesson.

The following day, Gopal was going to the temple as usual. On his way, he met a poor Brahmin named Dayasagar, who knew Gopal casually and had come to Krishnanagar after attending the *Kenduli Mela*[1]. After greeting each other, Gopal said to Dayasagar, "I am going to the temple for a *puja*[2]. But please go to my home, and I will join you shortly. My wife will give you a meal."

Dayasagar was happy to hear this and without showing any resistance, he merrily headed towards Gopal's home. When Gopal's wife saw this unwanted guest coming to their home, she patiently said, "Friend you are welcome to our place! But let me warn you about something. My husband has a peculiar habit of inviting people home for a meal, but then he takes my *'belan'*[3] (rolling pin) and my 'grinding stone', and beats them up till they scream for mercy."

Dayasagar was shocked to hear this. He got up quickly and said, "I forgot. . . I had to be in the next village for a ceremony. If I don't leave immediately I shall be late." And he rushed out.

---

1. *It is a fair held at Kenduli (Birbhum) on the occasion of Makar Sankranti (mid-January).*
2. *A religious ritual performed by Hindus as an offering to various deities.*
3. *'Belan' or 'rolling pin' is a cylindrical food preparation utensil (usually wooden) used to shape and flatten dough. It is a common item in every Indian kitchen.*

Gopal, on his way back from his *puja*, saw the guest rushing away and was puzzled. He hurried back home and asked his wife, "What happened to our guest?"

"He was a strange man," said his wife, "I offered him a meal but he said he wanted my *'belan'* and 'grinding stone'. I refused to give them to him and he rushed out in a temper."

"Why did you refuse?" cried Gopal, "He may have needed them for some important reason. Give them to me at once."

Grabbing the '*belan*' and the 'grinding stone', Gopal rushed after the guest. "Wait, wait," he cried, "I have the '*belan*' and the 'grinding stone' for you."

Hearing the words '*belan*' and 'grinding stone', Dayasagar ran even faster and soon disappeared from view. The confused Gopal never invited strangers to his home ever again.

Popular Version

Judgements, criticisms and opinions are the by-product of the thought process. Thought is powerful. Don't be hasty in facing situations, but be soft and gentle in your perception to know the facts and tackle the situation thoughtfully. You should neither be a product of rumors nor do you have to be a prisoner of rumors while tackling odd situations. Wise are those who tackle explosive situations thoughtfully, thus saving themselves from the trammels of confrontation.

Brazen Attack

Fact of the matter

To experience an experience is the ultimate experience. Life is a series of experiences. These experiences are a process. To flow with the process is being intelligent.

Fact Unfolded

One night, after Gopal Bhand and his wife had gone to bed, they heard some strange sounds.

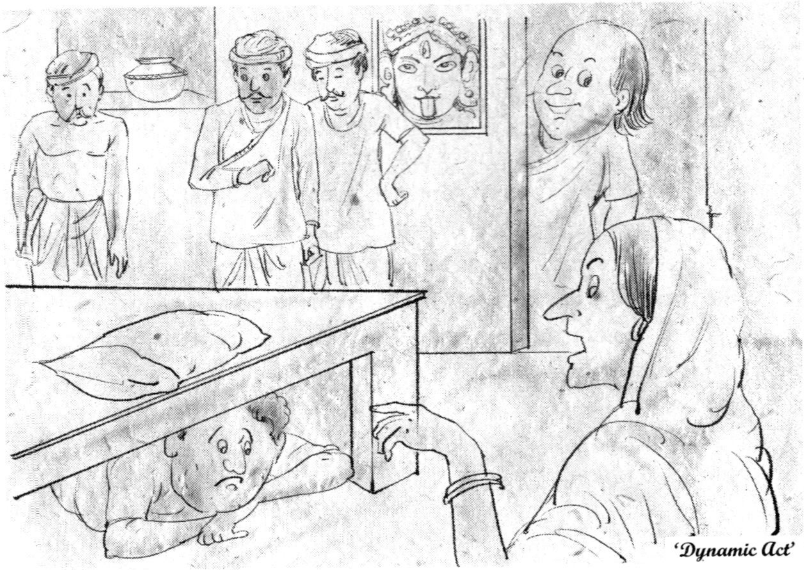

"It's a thief!" whispered his wife, frightened.

"Shhhhh...!" said Gopal, waiting to see if anyone broke into the house.

Bang! Crash!

The door burst open, and a rugged man rushed in carrying a huge knife.

"Quick!" he said, "Hand over all your jewels and valuables to me without making any noise. Hurry up, or I'll stab you!!"

"Here, you can have what you like," said Gopal's wife, terrified, "just don't kill us! You can have everything."

Suddenly, there was another loud sound from outside.

"Who's that?" shouted the thief, rattled.

"Maybe it's another thief, just like you," replied Gopal, calmly.

"Silence!" said the thief, listening to the sounds attentively, "Oh, my God!" he wailed.

"Who is it?" asked Gopal, politely, "Anyone you know?"

"I'm finished," said the thief. "It's the notorious Satrajit and his terrible gang of robbers from Gayespur!"

"Don't worry," said Gopal, "hide under this bed. I will deal with them, and let you know when they are gone."

And so the thief dived under the bed.

Before the gang of robbers stormed into Gopal's house, he quickly whispered some instructions to his wife, and walked out of the back door.

The gang of robbers entered and found only the lady of the house, shirking in a corner.

"Hey, you!" shouted Satrajit the gang leader, "Make this easy for yourself. Give us all your jewels and valuables or we'll kill you!"

"I can't," trembled Gopal's wife.

"Why not?" thundered Satrajit, the chief robber.

"They're all locked up, and the keys are with the master of the house," said the shivering woman.

"Where's he?" said Satrajit, "Hurry up!"

Gopal's wife pointed under the bed, "He's hiding in there," she said in a shaking tone.

The robbers dragged out the helpless thief from under the bed and beat him up. "Hand over the keys or we'll kill you! At Once!" they yelled.

"But I don't have them," wailed the thief, "I'm not the master of this house!"

"You cowardly liar! What will you say next? That this is not your wife?" roared Satrajit, beating the thief harshly once more.

Meanwhile, Gopal returned with the King's soldiers who surrounded the house and arrested the robbers.

"Where's the first thief?" the royal soldiers asked.

"I think he has learnt his lesson," replied Gopal smilingly and let the first thief go away.

In this way, the clever Gopal saved his life and property.

Popular Version

By thinking small, we remain small. Thinking in a new way will open life in a new perspective. Growth oriented thinking allows us to grow. When Walt Disney looked at a mouse in a new perspective, he got the idea of Mickey Mouse and the rest is history. Similarly, we should look at situations with a new perspective.

Cause for Celebration

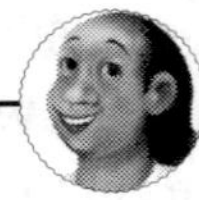

Fact of the Matter

More than the fact, it is the interpretation of the fact that teaches.

Fact Unfolded

In Krishnanagar, a wicked cobbler named Shirshendu lived close to Gopal's house. Shirshendu was dishonest and always made a fool of people who came to him for getting their footwear mended or prepared. He charged hefty amounts for petty works and offered cheap footwear to the public at exorbitant rates. Even if the footwear

'In his Words'

required petty repairs, he advised to get them changed for new ones and that too from him only.

The people of Krishnanagar were fed up with the crooked acts of Shirshendu. Once, Gopal thought of teaching him a lesson. He asked the crafty cobbler to make him a pair of *chappals*[1] – good, durable and strong enough to last for years. For such, Gopal promised to make Shirshendu happy.

Thinking it to be a good bargain, Shirshendu made a fine pair of *chappals*, gave them to Gopal and waited patiently for his money. But Gopal did not give the money to the cobbler. Every time he saw Gopal, he expected his money but Gopal would chat and walk on, and say nothing about the money he owed to Shirshendu.

One day Shirshendu decided to ask Gopal for the money. "I have already waited for three months," he said to Gopal, "I am not a rich man. Please pay me the cost of those *chappals* I made for you."

"Don't be impatient," said Gopal politely, "I promised you, one day I will make you happy."

The next time when both met, Shirshendu again asked Gopal for his money. At this, Gopal said, "You know the *taluqdar*[2]? He has just had a son. Does that make you happy?"

Shirshendu was puzzled by this question. If the cobbler said that he was not happy with the news, he could face the *taluqdar's* anger; otherwise he would lose the money. In the circumstances he shrugged his shoulders and simply replied, "Yes, I have been made very happy with this good news."

---

1. *Chappals or flip-flops are a common type of outdoor footwear in India and other Asian countries.*
2. *Indian land holders during Mughal and British times, responsible for maintaining law & order besides collecting taxes from a province.*

"There you are, then," said Gopal, "didn't I tell you that I would certainly make you happy one day?" And he walked away smilingly.

The poor cobbler knew how cleverly Gopal had made a fool of him and taught a lesson, but there was nothing he could do about it.

Popular Version

No one can go back and make a brand new start. Anyone can start from now and make a brand new ending.

❋❋❋

Between the Lies

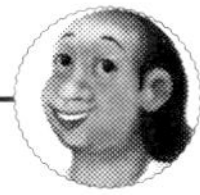

Fact of the Matter

We are experts in justifying our follies.

Fact Unfolded

Kamod was a poor fellow who used to sell hand fans made of palm leaves in Krishnanagar. To sell his fans, he usually proclaimed loud, 'This fan is long lasting, it will last a 100 years. So the price is 5 gold coins each. . .' That way, he managed to sell a few fans everyday to earn his livelihood.

Once, Kamod happened to sell his fans outside the Palace gates. Just then, Raja Krishna Chandra Rai with his entourage passed

'Anti Climax'

across Kamod. While passing, he heard Kamod's proclamation about the long lasting fans. The King felt amused. He immediately called Kamod into the *Rajbari*[1] and said, "Hey! Are you joking? How can this flimsy fan cost 5 gold coins? It should not cost more than a *cowrie*[2]! On top of it, you say it will last for a 100 years. What a bluff?"

Kamod said, "Oh King, this is a very rare fan. It can last for a 100 years. That is why the price is so high!" The King refused to accept his explanation; but the hawker went on pursuing. Finally the King gave up. The King agreed to buy a fan on the condition that if it failed to last a 100 years, he would cut the hawker's head off!

Thus the King bought a fan from Kamod for 5 gold coins. Later, as expected, the fan tore within a few hours.

The agitated King's men went looking for the hawker and brought him to the *Rajbari*. The King ordered him to be killed at once.

Hearing the punishment, Kamod was taken aback. He pleaded, "Oh King? I am a poor hawker. Please pardon me. Don't give me such a harsh punishment for a trivial proclamation."

But the King was adamant and threw Kamod in prison. He ordered that Kamod be killed after a week.

When Kamod's wife came to know of the King's harsh act, she was shattered. She wept and just wept. The dejected lady at last went to Gopal Bhand and explained the entire episode to him.

Gopal consoled the lady and assured to help her.

---

1. *The Royal Court/Palace*
2. *Cowrie (Kauri) is a glossy bright shell of any marine molluscs. It was used as money in many parts of South Asia during ancient and medieval periods. It was the smallest unit of coin in the currency.*

That day, Gopal went to the prison and met Kamod. He felt remorseful to see Kamod. Next day was fixed for Kamod's death. Gopal talked to Kamod and advised him to do as per his plan.

Kamod was totally broken and was unwilling to listen to anything. But when Gopal repeatedly assured to help him, Kamod had no option but to agree to Gopal's plan.

Next day, when Kamod was produced in front of the King in the *Rajbari*, he said, "Oh King! I am not afraid to die. But I really wonder as to how the fan that should have lasted at least 100 years, tore within such a short time in your hand! So, before killing me, I have my last wish. Would you be kind enough to explain it to me as to how you used that fan?"

The King relented to his last wish and showed him how he used the fan. At this, Kamod exclaimed with a hurt look, "Oh, no! This is where the whole mistake is! This fan would have surely lasted for at least 100 years... But this is not the way to use it. One should keep the fan in front and shake one's face to and fro and not the fan. Then the fan would certainly last for 100 years."

The King just laughed at Kamod's explanation and so did the courtiers and Gopal. Kamod was freed and he went straight to Gopal to thank him for his advice which saved his life.

Popular Version

We often create maps of people and want people to fit into our maps. Another bad habit that we possess is the inability to correct our errors easily. Though we know that the mistake is ours, we justify our actions. The bigger joke is in considering ourselves very clever for being able to justify our mistakes effectively!

Thought for Today

Fact of the Matter

At work, you need to be objective in your perception in order to be effective.

Fact Unfolded

One fine day, Gopal Bhand went to the public bathhouse for a refreshing massage and a bath. But unexpectedly, the servants at the bathhouse acted carelessly and didn't massage Gopal with the sponge. In that regard, when coming out, Gopal gave the bath's owner

all 10 gold coins he had. When the servants saw his generosity, they got embarrassed as to why they showed him such carelessness.

The next week, Gopal again went to the hot bath. This time all the servants gave him a splendid massage followed by a bath, all with extreme respect and honour, and showed extreme open-heartedness. But besides all this hard work and effort, Gopal gave only one gold coin to them when he came out.

The bath's workers angrily asked, "Last week you gave us unnecessary tip. But what is the reason for today's rude behaviour?"

Gopal replied, "I paid for today's bath last week when I came and gave the tip to you; I am paying for that bath today so that you people learn to behave respectfully with all your customers without any greed."

Listening to Gopal's comments, the workers realised their mistake and felt embarrassed.

Popular Version

Some continue to change jobs, mates and friends but never think of changing their own perception towards work. To change the perception, one has to observe oneself minutely and discreetly. So take the responsibility to develop the ability to change one's perception towards work instead of rejecting objective truths, theories, logic, universals, consensus, foundations, and scientific ideas.

A Progressive Decision

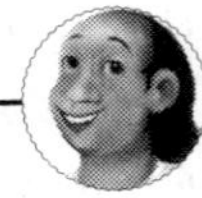

Fact of the Matter

Better be with enlightened people in prison than fools in paradise.

Fact Unfolded

Dwijesh was Gopal Bhand's close friend having a lucrative business of selling fish. Once, Dwijesh had to go to distant Ranaghat town to attend a wedding. While going on tour, Dwijesh entrusted the affairs of his shop to Gopal and expected the affairs to be managed appropriately by him.

'Myth-Making'

Gopal did his job meticulously. A routine customer noticed Gopal's intelligence in managing the dealings at the shop and got impressed.

"Tell me Gopal, what makes you so smart?" the customer curiously asked one day.

"I wouldn't share my secret with just anyone," Gopal replied, lowering his voice so that the other shoppers won't hear. "But since you're a good and faithful customer, I'll definitely tell you. . . . *Fish Heads*. You see, they are an excellent source of my brainpower. You eat enough of them and you'll be positively brilliant."

"You sell them here?" the customer asked.

"Yes ... off course. Four pieces for a gold coin only," said Gopal.

The customer bought twelve. A week later, the customer came to Gopal and complained that the *Fish Heads* were disgusting and he wasn't any smarter.

"You didn't eat enough," adviced Gopal. The customer went home with twenty more *Fish Heads*. Two weeks later, he again came to Gopal and this time he was really angry.

"Hey Gopal," he complained, "you're selling me four *Fish Heads* for one gold coin when I can easily buy a full grown succulent *hilsha*[1] for a coin. You're ripping me off! And those *Fish Heads* didn't make me any smarter either," the customer continued to explain angrily.

"You see?" said Gopal, "You're smarter already." Saying this, Gopal passed his usual half smile to the dumbfounded customer.

---

1. A popular oily and tropical fish.

Popular Version

Hug each moment of life to give yourself a break and start seeing things differently.

❋❋❋

The Legacy of the Jester continues. . .

Droplets of Wisdom

Gopal Bhand was certainly not the usual kind of hero. The usual kind of hero is somewhat brave in battle, wins a beautiful princess's hand in marriage, and rules his Kingdom well. He fights lions and tigers, and comes home unscathed.

Gopal was just a barber but a clever one indeed. All he did was shave well, give young men good haircut, and massage their head so well that everyone thought they were in heaven.

But certainly Gopal was not an ordinary barber. He was tremendously witty and wise. And it was for these qualities that he was

'Crowning Glory of the Rajbari'

Raja Krishna Chandra Rai's personal barber and favourite royal jester. The King was taken over by the intelligence and charm of Gopal.

Gopal proved to be of immense support to the Emperor to deal with odd situations often posed by *Nawab Siraj-ud-Daula*, *Mir Kasim* and the *Marathas*[1] who were a persistent nuisance to Raja Krishna Chandra.

But still, there were certain courtiers and subjects, who disliked Gopal. They made mockery of the King's overconfidence towards Gopal.

One day, the King was so much fed up with the envy of the courtiers towards Gopal that he made a loud public announcement, "I perceive that my Court jester Gopal is the most intelligent person in the whole world. Of course, to prove this, Gopal can be put to test any time. Whoever asks Gopal a question on whatever subject, he will answer; never mind even if the toughest of questions are posed to him!"

This sudden claim caused ripples all across the Empire and adjoining Kingdoms. The *Nawab* of *Murshidabad*, the biggest rival of *Raja* Rai also heard about the King's challenge. He found this to be an excellent occasion to humiliate Raja Rai. He too immediately ordered his distinguished scholars to accompany him to the *Rajbari*[2] to test the King's claim about his jester.

The *Nawab* expressed his desire to verify the jester's intelligence and so did the *Rajbari* courtiers.

So a day was fixed for the challenge and to test Gopal's unmatched wit. Everyone gathered in the *Rajbari* in excitement. The *Nawab* also arrived in the *Rajbari* alongwith his *Begam*[3] and distinguished scholars.

---

1. *Nawab Siraj-ud-Daula, Mir Kasim and the Marathas were Raja's chief political rivals*
2. *The Royal Court/Palace.*
3. *Queen*

Grand arrangements were made. A huge *shamiana*[4] was raised in the wide *angina*[5] of the Palace. The Royal *mali*[6] decorated the whole pandaal with the best of fragrant flowers – *champak*, *parul*, *aparajita* and *ketuki*. Choicest of cuisine were prepared and laid out to the guests.

The King sent for Gopal. He arrived. He was still bewildered with the King's announcement but he was more surprised to see the grand crowd and their anxiety for the occasion.

Everybody was seated in the *Rajbari* – His Majesty Raja Krishna Chandra Rai, Rani Bhabani, Robert Clive, *Nawab* of *Murshiadabad*, *Nawab's Begam*, *mantris*[7], courtiers, scholars and dignitaries.

Puja[8] was performed in front of a huge idol of *Maa Kali*. *Sholakas*[9] read out amidst blowing of conch shell by the *Rajguru Purohit*[10]. The rules of the challenge were read out. Raja Rai, Rani Bhabani, Robert Clive, *Nawab* and distinguished scholars would pose questions on whatsoever subject – religion, theology, warfare, philosophy, mythology, and so on and Gopal would have to field them. Anybody from the public audience was also allowed to put questions to Gopal.

So the question and answer session begun. Gopal clad in a silken *dhoti-kurta* with a *gamcha* on his shoulders and a *chappal* in the feet, sat on a high chair placed in the centre, surrounded by the dignitaries all around. Gopal keenly stared the onlookers.

---

4. Tent
5. Courtyard
6. Gardener
7. Ministers
8. Worship)
9. Religious Sanskrit couplets
10.Royal Priest

A pin-drop silence prevailed.

"Well, Sire, this is the first question," asked the *Nawab's Wazir*[11] to Gopal,"Can you tell me how much water the Bay of Bengal holds?"

Gopal stood up, bowed low in front of the King and the dignitaries to seek their blessings. Politely seeking permission to speak, Gopal modestly answered,"Sire, if you please stop the tides ... I'll be happy to measure it for you!"

The audience applauded at Gopal's maiden reply.

The *Qazi*[12] of the *Nawab* stepped forward and asked, "How many days ago did God create the earth?"

"Seven," said Gopal, without hesitating. "For when seven days pass, another seven days begin. . . ."

"All right," said the *Nawab's Talukdaar*[13]. "You seem to know the answers to all questions. Tell me where the centre of the earth is!"

"Right here, of course. Take a long rope and measure the earth. You'll see I'm right!" Gopal said.

"Well, then," again said the *Nawab's Qazi*. "How far is it from here to heaven?"

"Very close," replied the barber. "Try praying as softly as you can. Your prayers will be heard in heaven!"

Listening to the brain-storming session, everyone in the *Rajbari* gave a standing ovation to Gopal. So everyone had to agree that Gopal was indeed as smart as the King claimed. The King was seen

---

11.Ministers
12. Muslim Priest
13. Chief

relaxing confidently enjoying the session.

The curious *Nawab* went a bit forward to ask, "Gopal you say you know everything in the world, then tell me which animals lay eggs and which animals give birth to their young ones."

Gopal looked back at him, smiled and said, "The animals that have their 'EARS' outside their body gives birth to their young ones and the animals that have their 'EARS' inside their body lay eggs."

The dumbfounded *Nawab* continued to ask, "Okay, answer a simple riddle. . . 'You cannot see him in the same way as you see others. His voice is different than what you hear. He is always with you when you are alone or in a crowd. He listens to each and every word you utter and he is your best friend but speaks to you once in a blue moon... Who's he?'"

After thinking for a while and tabbing his belly, Gopal softly replied, "YOURSELF."

The session went a step ahead raising the thrill even more. The excitement could be noticed on everybody's face in the *Rajbari*.

The *Nawab's* jester stood forward. With mouth full of *paan*, he gathered courage and asked, "Ok Gopal. . . Here is a puzzle ...'A man went on a trip with a fox, a goose, and a sack of corn. He came upon a stream which he had to cross and found a tiny boat to use to cross the stream. He could only take himself and one other – the fox, the goose, or the corn – at a time. He could not leave the fox alone with the goose because the fox will eat the goose. Or he could not leave the goose alone with the corn because the goose will feed upon the entire corn. The man is in a total confusion. Now tell, how will the man manage the situation and get all safely over the stream'?"

After a brief silence, Gopal replied, "First the man should take the goose over the stream in a boat, leave it there and come back alone. Then he should take the fox over the stream in the boat, leave it there and bring the goose back. Now he should leave the goose there, take the corn over the stream in the boat and come back alone to get the goose. Finally he should take the goose over and the job will be done!"

Nawab's Dalpati[14] stepped forward to ask, "Gopal you like fishing. Isn't it? Then answer my simple question. 2 fathers and 2 sons go fishing. Each of them catches one fish. But why do they bring home only 3 fish?"

"Because, the group consisted of grandfather, father and son," answered Gopal.

With each question, the excitement further grew.

Gopal was further asked by a *Saudagar*[15] from *Murshidabad*, "Which one is greater, the *Nawab* or the peasant?"

Gopal said, "Obviously the peasant is greater because if he didn't plant wheat, then the *Nawab* would die of hunger."

"Now a tough question that you won't be able to answer," said *Nawab's mantri.* "Gopal, tell me a number, that if we divide it by any number from 1-10, the answer will always come in the form of a whole number and not a fraction."

Gopal looked back at him and said, "Take the number of days in a year and multiply it with the number of days in a week and you will have your answer."

---

14. Leader of a Battalion
15. an effluent trader

The *mantri* got astonished but calculated the answer as Gopal gave him. To his amazement he got the right answer and came across the following results:

The number of Days in a Year = 360
The Number of Days in a Week = 7
The product of the two numbers = 2,520

Now . . .
2520 ÷ 1 = 2520
2520 ÷ 2 = 1260
2520 ÷ 3 = 840
....
....
2520 ÷ 10= 252*

The question and answer session could not be completed during day one. So it was adjourned for day two.

That night, the whole city was abuzz with enthusiasm. But more than the zeal, the people were curious about the results of the test. Everybody wanted their King and the clever jester to win the challenge with flying colours. After all, it was a matter of prestige of the *Raja* and his *Rajbari* for centuries to come.

Then, started day two of the test amidst more excitement than the day one.

Everybody occupied their seats in the *Rajbari*.

---

* *In medieval periods, Arabic system of numbers was followed which prescribed 360 days in a year*
2520 ÷ 1 = 2520 *2520 ÷ 2 = 1260* *2520 ÷ 3 = 840*
2520 ÷ 4 = 630
2520 ÷ 5 = 504 *2520 ÷ 6 = 420* *2520 ÷ 7 = 360*
2520 ÷ 8 = 315
2520 ÷ 9 = 280 *2520 ÷ 10=252*

After the usual *puja*, again a volley of questions was posed to Gopal, who sat in the middle with curious eyes.

The *Nawab's Wazir* asked,"Which tree is it that has an age of one year, have twelve branches and on each branch there are thirty leaves, one direction facing light while the other faces toward darkness?"

Gopal immediately replied, "This tree represents the year, the month, and day and night because there are 12 months in a year and 30 days in a month, which are half day and half night."

The *Nawab's Qazi* came to Gopal and said, "Prove to me the existence of God."

Gopal requested him to be seated.

Just at that time, Gopal saw an attendant carrying a tray of hen's eggs towards the Royal kitchen. Gopal called the attendant and took an egg from him. Gopal kept the egg on his palm. Then pointing towards the egg, he told, "See, it is such a strong fort that has no doors. On its outside is a hard skin and below it is a thin membrane, inside which flows two seas of yellow and white. But neither can the yellow sea mix with the white nor the white sea can merge with the yellow. Neither can a repairer enter it nor does a destroyer come out of it. No one can even know whether the newborn would be a male or a female.

Then all of a sudden it cracks and a beautiful chick emerges from it. Can your reason agree that all this happened without a designer or a maker?" Hearing this, the *Qazi* bowed down his head and said, "I appreciate Gopal's astuteness."

The session gained more momentum. The scholars of the *Rajbari* including the *Raja* and *Rani* also tested their jester.

"Gopal! What is that which you can fly the highest?" asked Bharatchandra, the *Raja's* court poet.

"Imagination is the highest kite that one can fly," replied Gopal.

Bhabananda Majumdar, another scholar of the *Rajbari* asked, "What is the greatest of all things?"

"Space is the greatest of all things," said Gopal, "for space contains all that has been created."

"Which are more numerous – the living or the dead?" Ramprasad

Sen, another courtier of the *Rajbari* asked Gopal. "The living," said Gopal, "because the dead no longer count."

"And what is the best of all things?" the *Rajbari* courtier Pandit Baneswar Bidyalankar asked.

"Virtue," replied Gopal. "There is nothing better than virtue."

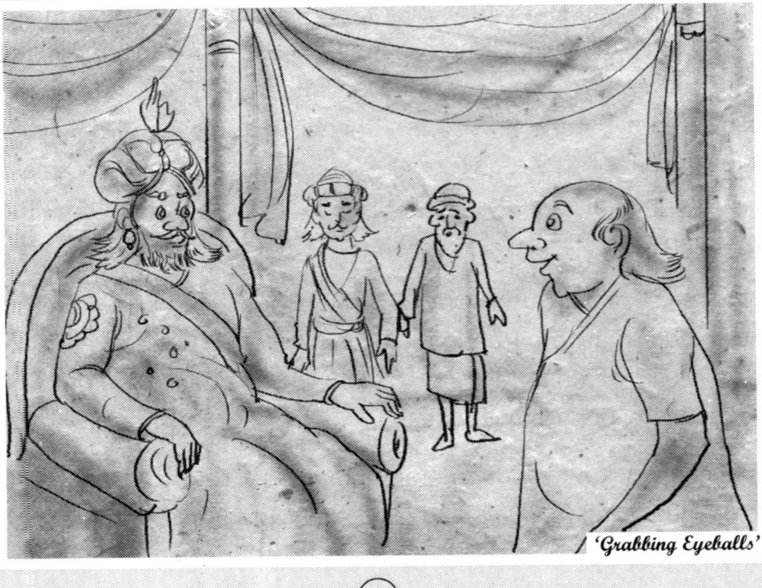

'Grabbing Eyeballs'

“What is the quickest of all things?” another scholar of the *Rajbari* Krishnananda Bachaspati raised.

“Thought. For thoughts can fly to the end of the universe within a split second,” answered Gopal.

The questions continued to be showered one after the other. The scholar Jagannath Tarkapanchanan enquired, “What is the easiest of all things?”

“To give advice ... To give advice to another and not to act upon it is perhaps the easiest of all things.”

“And what is the most difficult of all things?” the scholar Hariram Tarkasiddhanta asked.

And Gopal answered, “To know oneself!”

“What does a man have to do to become a God?” a *Sanyasi*[16] from the audience asked Gopal, who responded, “Do what is impossible for a man.”

The petite Rani Bhabani keenly observing the entire session politely asked, “There are four brothers in this world that were all born together. The first runs and never tires. The second eats and is never full. The third drinks and is always thirsty. The fourth sings a song that is never good. Please name these four brothers Gopal.”

Gopal bowed before the *Rani* and replied softly, “Madam. . . These four brothers are none else than – water, fire, earth and wind.”

“Which produces more creatures, the sea or the land?” *Rajguru Purohit* asked Gopal. “The land,” was Gopal’s answer, “because the sea is only a part of it.”

---

16. A holy hermit

Gopal was further asked by the *Senapati*[17], "Which animal is the smartest of all?" and Gopal replied with a smile, "The one we have not found yet."

The *Senapati* further asked, "What argument he and his King had used to stir up the Hindus to fight the *Marathas*?" To this, Gopal answered enthusiastically, "Only that one should either live nobly or die nobly."

"What should a man do to make himself loved?" asked the *Nawab's Begam*. To this Gopal replied, "Be powerful without being frightening."

The next question was asked by the *Nawab's Kotwal*[18], "Which is stronger? Whether it is death or life?" and Gopal answered, "Life is stronger than death, because it bears so many miseries, turmoil and pain."

Even Robert Clive could not stop his curiosity. He asked, "Gopal! Can you please name three consecutive days of the week without using the words Wednesday, Friday or Sunday?"

"Sure Sire, the three consecutive days are yesterday, today and tomorrow."

"Who is superior in the world? Animals or human beings?" again asked Robert Clive.

"Of course animals are superior to human beings. There are thirty horses in a race and fifty thousand people go to see it; but put thirty people in a race and not one horse would go to see it," Gopal replied thoughtfully.

---

17. Army Commander
18. Police Chief

"My neighbour Dilshad's father has six sons who are named fantastically — January, February, March, April, May .... What is the name of sixth son?" asked Clive once again.

"June? Well no? Dilshad, because he is the sixth son," said Gopal mopping his brow carefully.

"It took 10,000 workers to build the *Sonar Gouranga Mandarim* at *Nawabdip*[19] in 10 years. Now tell me, how many workers would be required to build it in 5 years?" asked the Royal *Khazanchi*[20].

Gopal stopped for a while, shook his head and said, "You know that I am a bit week in mathematics. Anyway, how come the *Sonar Gouranga Mandarim* be built in 5 years. .. It is already built."

"Gopal you are a distinguished barber. Isn't it? Then tell me what do you have for graying hair?" asked a *Hakim*[21] from the audience.

"Nothing but the highest respect Sire," Gopal answered.

"Which is the deepest trench in the world?" asked the Nawab's *Begam* and the answer was, "A woman's heart."

She further asked, "Who is a man's best friend?" and Gopal answered, "His own good sense."

The *Nawab* who was listening carefully leaned closer. He said, "I shall either ask you ten easy questions or one really difficult question. Think well before you make up your mind!" Gopal thought for a while and said, "My choice is one really difficult question."

---

19. The Sonar Gouranga Mandiram is one of the most famous temples in Nabadwip. The temple is a grand structure and has the Golden Shrine of Shri Chaitanya Mahaprabhu. His footwear has been kept here, in a glass case.

20. Treasurer

21. Physician

"Well, good luck to you, you have made your own choice! Now tell me this. What comes first — Day or Night?" the *Nawab* asked curiously.

Gopal nodded . . . thought for a while and said, "It's the Day, Sire!" came the reply.

"How?" said the *Nawab*, swallowing hard.

"Sorry Sire, you promised me that you will not ask me a SECOND difficult question!" said Gopal promptly leaving the *Nawab* and everyone in the *Rajbari* amazed.

Everybody cheered thumping their chests proudly.

Gopal satisfied everyone. None had any doubts for Gopal's unmatched wit. Everyone admitted that the King was absolutely right in having utmost faith and confidence in Gopal.

Everybody seated in the *Rajbari* admired the quick wit Gopal possessed and acknowledged the intelligence of Gopal beyond doubt. Not only the King, but the *Nawab* bestowed rewards upon Gopal Bhand. Gopal again proved his intelligence and not only did he saved the prestige of the Empire but also supported the King's claim towards Gopal's unparallel wit.

An Inbox

So it can be conveniently seen that the very meaning of being alive is to be constantly in the process of becoming a new creation. Somewhere deep down, we all are filled with a mystical longing, a yearning for ultimate meaningfulness, and therefore, we need to see our entire world in that context.

Gopal Bhand with his unmatched comic confidence and intelligence always proved to be a winner amongst all the stiff-necked courtiers. His inquisitiveness, ever ready eagerness to face problems and vivid wit brilliantly depicted the many layers of his persona.

Gopal's account of anecdotes provides an all-round understanding to manage our problems and comprehend various aspects of life in a meaningful manner. Gopal's strategic traits to manage the problems can be brewed as the following commandments:

1. Agree that **HONESTY** is a priority.
2. Aim for **PROGRESS** with **PERFECTION**.
3. In every honest relationship, a few **WHITE LIES** are okay.
4. Follow the **KARMIC ARITHMETIC**. Two wrongs do not make a right. That's Arithmetic. Two negative numbers total up to a bigger negative number; a positive number when added to a negative number reduces the negativity.
5. Have **WISDOM** with **COMPASSION**, i.e. *Frajana* with *Karuna*.
6. For unalloyed **JOY**, add to Gandhiji's three monkeys – *Mizaru* (see no evil), *Kikazaru* (hear no evil) and *Iwazaru* (speak no

evil); the forth monkey *Shizaru* (do no evil).

7. **SHARING** and **CARING** gives more joy than just accumulating material wealth. The former King of Bhutan had nicely put it in this way: 'Gross National Happiness is what matters; not Gross National Product.'
8. Cultivate the belief that the universe is **FRIENDLY**, that life is **BENEVOLENT**, that good things will happen to us and that even if bad things happen; they can make us better and wiser!
9. Our **BODY, MIND** and **INTELLECT** are amazing **GIFTS**, and we need to put them to the best possible use.
10. Our **WELFARE** is in the **WELFARE** of all. To live in harmony, attempt a conscious effort to make **SELF-INQUIRY** a **HABIT**.
11. **FOCUSSING** on Thoughts – slowly and gradually will overpower our negative thoughts arising in our mind which makes it jump like a monkey from one thought to another.
12. Doing **GOOD** to the whole world is the primary objective. **GREED** is behind every **DESIRE**. So, we need to start saying 'no'. Be ready to accept **TRUTH** and give up **UNTRUTH**.
13. Act according to the dictates of **DHARMA**, after due reflection over right and wrong. Promote *vidya* or knowledge and dispel *avidya* or ignorance.
14. Turn everything that happens in your life towards your **EVOLUTION** by just being **CONSCIOUS**.
15. **MORALITY** is what moulds you. Irrespective of the fact whether we expect things or not, the truth is that every cause has an effect. In other words, we may continue to act in the most unselfish and moral manner but the effect of the act is never lost.
16. **WORRY** will enter the mind, but you must refuse to entertain

it. Do not say 'yes' to worry. Say 'no' to worry and to all the sorrows in your life. Refuse to be miserable. That life's secret.

17. Make the shift from **NEGATIVISM** to **POSITIVISM**, from **SELF-CONDEMNATION** to **SELF-ELEVATION**. Start thinking about the beautiful, pleasant and expansive nature of the mind. Share your happiness with others – instead of hoarding it all for yourself.
18. **THOUGHT** is energy. Every thought vibrates at its uniquely powerful frequency. . . . Positive thoughts lift up our energy fields, and negative thoughts drag it down.
19. The many **QUALITIES** and **FEELINGS** (*bhavs*) that Nature has given to us should be preserved. So wipe your slate clean to learn more.
20. Accept that life is a cycle of **PAIN** and **PLEASURE**. We cannot escape pain. When we accept this, then we start changing, and start thinking how to live with the pain.
21. **CRYSTALLISE** your **AIM** by believing that everything happens for a reason.
22. Consider each moment in life as the **FINAL ONE**, so you use every moment to the fullest.

The above commandments if adopted genuinely and appropriately during adverse times are enough to help a person transform and face the situation in a better manner instead of venting negative emotions. These traits need to be imbibed to make one learn to grow in adverse situations instead of being defeated by them. Or they are enough to help us **'MANAGE OUR PROBLEMS'** neatly.

Author: Prof. Shrikant Prasoon
Format: Paperback
Language: English
Pages: 248

Chanakya was both a destructive and creative thinker able to annihilate an established empire and erect and establish another larger, richer and greater on the debris, without money, material and man. So, he is the only qualified person in human history to be Guru; Acharya; Teacher; Guide and Mentor in the field of Management. With his super mind and supreme determination he succeeded in everything and everywhere; and wrote down everything without inhibitions or secrecy for the posterity in his three monumental works:

1. Teachings of Kautilya's Arthashastra & Nitishastra
2. Perfect Analogy between Ancient Managerial System & Modern Corporate Setup

(Also available in Hindi)

Author: Vishal Goyal
Format: Paperback
Language: English
Pages: 228

Tenali Raman was a court jester, an intelligent advisor and one of the ashtadiggajas (elephants serving as pillars and taking care of all the eight sides) in the Bhuvana Vijayam (Royal Court) of the famed Emperor of Vijayanagar Empire (City of Joy) in Karnataka – Sri Krishna Deva Raya (1509-1529), the model ruler par excellence to Ashoka, Samudra Gupta and Harsha Vardhana. Tenali Raman was an embodiment of acute wit and humour and an admirable poet of knowledge, shrewdness and ingenuity. In a short span, the legacy left behind by Tenali Raman attained eternity. All these qualities of Tenali Raman have been fully explored and displayed in this collection of vibrant fables and anecdotes.

Author: S.P. Sharma
Format: Paperback
Language: English
Pages: 256

This book gives a vivid description of Chanakya's doctrines, as written in his famous book, Arthashastra. The entire content has been taken from the original book but simplified and explained in an easy language for the common man. There are 17 chapters in the book containing the true essence of an ideal administrative system, the duties and responsibilities of an able ruler, how to become an efficient ruler, how to govern, the basic principles of a good government, how to strengthen the political and physical boundaries of a kingdom/government, how to increase the wealth of a kingdom/government or improve its economy and bring forth prosperity, which is relevant even today for good governance.

Author: Bittu Kumar
Format: Paperback
Language: English
Pages: 136

"The aim of marketing is to know and understand the customer so well, the product or service fits him and sells itself,"

– Peter F. Drucker

The book, Marketing for Beginners gives an exhaustive explanation about the key concepts of marketing, its strategies, and defines the important terminologies, such as Brand Selection, Distribution Channels, Vendor Selection, Pricing, Sales Process, Customer Relationship Management(CRM).

It's different and exclusive from other Marketing or Management books as it not only gives the detailed description of the various components of Marketing, but also cites examples to explain each of them, making it crystal clear to the readers.

Author: Anchit Barnwal
Format: Paperback
Language: English
Pages: 168

Just as a winning podium can accommodate anyone on it, each one of us is capable to be a winner, irrespective of our shortcomings and differences. Winners' Podium – Everyone Fits on it, attempts to do just that: make out a winner amongst each one of us.

This book offers elaborate guidelines for a balanced, successful and happy living. It tells how one can find his talent, attract ideas and be successful, both personally and professionally. It also talks of happiness and the steps to it.

Through stories, anecdotes, quotations, examples and day to day observations, this book can inspire you to not only attain that most desirable success, but also to hold on and grow both internally and externally with it.

Author: V. Rajesh
Format: Paperback
Language: English
Pages: 104

It is easy to skip a question during an exam if it is "Out of Syllabus" but what do you do if you are faced with a situation in life for which you were not given any inputs? Can you run away from the situation using the "Out of Syllabus" excuse?

Career is one area where one is expected to know and manage situations. After all a person is paid a salary to be able to handle things and deliver results. The reality is that most people get a lot of academic and conceptual inputs relating to one's career choice but very little practical inputs on how to effectively use the academic learning.

visit our online bookstore: **www.vspublishers.com**

Author: Saurabh Aggrwal
Format: Paperback
Language: English
Pages: 256

Did you know that crossword puzzles first appeared in the New York World in 1913, and soon became a popular feature in newspapers or that Kellog's as a brand had spent $90,000 on advertising, more than 100 years ago in 1906, including one $4000 a page ad in the July issue of the Ladies Home Journal, Apple - had lured John Sculley away from Pepsi because they wanted him to apply his marketing skills to the personal computer market. Find facts and trivia from the world of business that will amaze and delight you. The questions in this book have been framed in a way that they are: guessable with intelligent, lateral, or lucky thinking; interesting, amusing, or surprising;

Author: Manish Vohra
Format: Paperback
Language: English
Pages: 128

The book helps the reader to get access to wisdom of several scriptures in one piece. Several sutras which are normally only passed on in the oral tradition are documented in the book.

Just like a magician never reveals his secrets, psychics also never reveal their secrets. There are several books written by psychics but they never reveal their methods. This book not only reveals the methods but also contains several simple exercises to enhance intuitive perception.

Author: O.P. Sharma
Format: Paperback
Language: English
Pages: 144

Life is full of ups and downs. While we exhilarate in the 'ups', we are totally at a loss when it comes to dealing with the 'downs'. This book has been specifically designed to help you turn the tide in your favour in the face of odds. "Each day is a fresh day — look at it with hope and enthusiasm, yesterday is over." Whatever the situation, you can make the best of things by the right approach.

If you wish to rise in your career, begin liking your work. If you wish to excel, have a healthy approach to criticism. If you want to scare away failures, preserve your peace of mind in the face of heavy odds. If you desire a happy married life, learn to respect your spouse.

visit our online bookstore: **www.vspublishers.com**